JESUS

Personal Reflections Series

BETH
MOORE

JESUS

90 DAYS WITH THE ONE AND ONLY

B&H
PUBLISHING GROUP
NASHVILLE, TENNESSEE

ISBN: 978-0-8054-4645-6

B&H Publishing Group

Nashville, Tennessee

BHPublishingGroup.com

Dewey Decimal Classification: 232.9

Jesus Christ \ Christian Life \ Spiritual Formation

Unless otherwise stated, all Scripture passages are taken from the Holy Bible, New International Version® Copyright © 1973, 1978, 1984 International Bible Society. Used by permission of Zondervan. All rights reserved. Other versions cited include the King James Version (KJV).

All Scripture passages used in the "Stop and Consider" and "Praying God's Word Today" sections are taken from the Holman Christian Standard Bible (HCSB), copyright © 1999, 2000, 2002, 2003 by Holman Bible Publishers.

Printed in Belgium

1 2 3 4 10 09 08 07

In Memory of Marge Caldwell,

Marge was the first person whose passionate love for Jesus took my breath away.
I will never comprehend how I have been so blessed by God to have known her,
loved her, and to have learned from her. God so tightly knitted the threads of our
ministries together that I'm not sure where one ends and the other begins.
Something of Marge is lived out in me every single good day. She taught me
countless things, like how to be not only a woman in ministry but also a lady.
Her love for Jesus the One and Only was wildly contagious. I am only one of
many who caught it feverishly. A few days before Jesus swept her home, I leaned
over her bedside and tried once again to express my gratitude for all she invested
in me. Once again my words failed to articulate my heart. I loved her dearly.

Beth

He is Jesus.

The One and Only.

Transcendent over all else.

To know Him is to love Him.

To love Him is to long for Him.

To long for Him is to finally reach

soul hands into the One true thing

we need never get enough of.

Jesus.

Take all you want.

Take all you need.

Till soul is fed.

And spirit freed.

Till dust is dust.

And Face you see.

Jesus Christ.

He's all you need.

Introduction

I really struggled with the overwhelming task of writing a book on the life of Christ. First of all, others far brighter and more knowledgeable already filled the shelves of libraries. Second, I feared that human commentary might accomplish little more than a detraction from what the Gospels have already divinely stated. I found the task extremely intimidating from beginning to end. I distinctly recall my chief request of God when I began this book: "Just don't let me embarrass You!" Though God no doubt watches over every word of commentary voiced over Scripture, I can't help but think He's even more particular when the subject matter is His one and only Son.

That Son of His is the dearest thing in my whole life. I don't have pens or paper enough to express my gratitude for the privilege of knowing Him and loving Him. The little I know is so transforming and revolutionary to me that I yearn to know more. My chief request of God is that He will supernaturally flood my life with an unending, ever-increasing desire for His Son. Jesus is not only my delight; He is my safety. Loving Him with absolute abandon is no doubt in my own best interest. As one who has been delivered from a life of defeat and hidden self-destruction, my deepest desire for every man, woman, youth, and child is to find that love.

My romance with Jesus Christ began in a tiny circle of baby-bear chairs in a Sunday school class of a small town church. My teachers were not biblical scholars. They were moms and homemakers. I'm not sure they ever delved into the depths of Scripture or researched a single Greek word. They simply taught what they knew. I don't know any other way to explain what happened next: I believed.

I remember thinking how handsome Jesus was in those watercolor pictures. I also remember thinking that I had never seen a man with long hair before. I wondered if my daddy, the Army major, would approve. My favorite picture was the familiar one with the children climbing all over Jesus' lap. As I recall, it was the only one I ever saw that captured

Him smiling. I determined quickly that big people bored and upset Him, and little people made Him quite happy.

As I recount this simple, unexciting testimony to you, a lump wells in my throat. Tears burn in my eyes. Jesus is the most wonderful, most graceful, most exciting, most redemptive thing that has ever happened to me. He is my life. I cannot express on paper my love for Him. It is a love that has grown in incongruous bits and pieces, baby steps, leaps, bounds, tumbles, and falls . . . decade after decade.

A romance with Christ differs so dramatically from a romance between mortals. I do not wish any other woman to love my husband, Keith, the way I do. How differently my romance with Christ! I want *all* of you to love Him . . . at least as much as I do. I'm jealous for us to want Him more than we want blessing, health, or even breath. I want to know Him so well that my undivided heart can explain, "Because Your love is better than life, my lips will glorify You" (Ps. 63.3). *Better than life!* God invites mortal creatures—you and me—into a love relationship with the Son of glory. That, my friend, is the meaning of life. Let's partake. Fully. Completely.

We will never spend our time more valuably than in the pursuit of knowing Jesus Christ. My deepest prayer is that this offering would take you another step closer in the noblest pursuit of life. I have very little doubt I will leave more lacking in this particular book than any other book God has entrusted to me, simply because there is no end to what could be said—and indeed *must* be said—if not by mortal creatures, then by those invisible to our eyes, encircling the throne and singing in a loud voice, "Worthy is the Lamb!"

DAY 1

Give Him the Name Jesus

BEFORE YOU BEGIN
Read Luke 1:26–33

STOP AND CONSIDER
You will conceive and give birth to a son, and you will call His name Jesus (v. 31).

What other words come to mind when you hear or speak the name Jesus? What moods or emotions bubble to the surface? What hopes does He stir up in your spirit? Almighty, magnificant, awesome, etc. When I hear or speak the name of Jesus, my spirit gets excited. I know that He is in control of everything.

If you had been Mary, how do you think you might have responded to this pronouncement of His name, especially at this declaration of Mary's involvement in His birth?

I would probably be thinking, "what am I getting into" just to know what the name Jesus means.

Picture the omniscient eyes of the unfathomable *El Roi*—the God who sees—spanning the universe in panoramic view, every galaxy in His gaze. Imagine now the gradual tightening of His lens as if a movie camera were attached to the point of a rocket bound for planet Earth. Not a man-made rocket, but a celestial rocket—of the living kind.

Gabriel has been summoned once again to the throne of God. At least six months have passed since God last sent him to Jerusalem, to foretell another unexpected birth—this one to an elderly priest named Zechariah, whose equally aged wife, Elizabeth, was to bear a son, John—John the Baptist. This previous assignment took Gabriel to Herod's temple, one of the wonders of the civilized world. But this time heaven's lens focuses northward.

Imagine Gabriel plunging earthward through the floor of the third heaven, breaking the barrier from the supernatural to the natural world. Feature him swooping down through the second heaven past the stars God calls by name. As our vision "descends," the earth grows larger. God's kingdom gaze burns through the blue skies of planet Earth and plummets like a flaming stake in the ground to a backward town called Nazareth.

I love to imagine where Mary was when Gabriel appeared to her. I wonder if she was in her bedroom or walking a dusty path fetching water for her mother. One thing for sure: she was alone.

No matter where the angelic ambassador appeared to Mary, he must have stunned her with his choice of salutations: "Greetings, you who are highly favored! The Lord is with you." Prior to Zechariah's encounter, four centuries had passed since God had graced the earth with a heavenly visitation. I doubt the thought occurred to anyone that he would transmit the most glorious news ever heard in all the world to a simple Galilean girl.

How I love the way God works! Just when we decide He's too complicated to comprehend, He draws stick pictures.

I'm sure Mary wasn't looking for an angelic encounter that day. As the recipient of such news, she was totally unsuspecting. Humble. Meek. Completely caught off guard. Luke 1:29 tells us Mary was "greatly troubled" at his words. The phrase actually means "to stir up throughout." You know the feeling: when butterflies don't just flutter in your stomach but land like a bucket at your feet, splashing fear and adrenaline through every appendage. Mary felt the fear through and through, wondering what kind of greeting this might be. How could this young girl comprehend that she was "highly favored" (Luke 1:28) by the Lord God Himself?

> How I love the way God works! Just when we decide He's too complicated to comprehend, He draws stick pictures.

The angel's next statement was equally stunning: "The Lord is with you." Although similar words had been spoken over men such as Moses, Joshua, and Gideon, I'm not sure they had ever been spoken over a woman. I'm not suggesting the Lord is not as present in the lives of women as He is men, but this phrase suggested a unique presence and power for the purpose of fulfilling a divine kingdom plan. The sight of the young girl gripped by fear provoked Gabriel to continue with the words, "Do not be afraid, Mary, you have found favor with God" (v. 30). Not until his next words did she have any clue why he had come or for what she had been chosen.

"You will be with child and give birth to a son" (v. 31). Not just any son—"the Son of the Most High" (v. 32). Probably only Mary's youth and inability to absorb the information kept her from fainting in a heap!

Then came my favorite line of all: "You are to give him the name Jesus" (v. 31). Do you realize this was the first proclamation of our Savior's personal name since the beginning of time? Jesus. The very name at which every knee will one day bow. The very name that every tongue will one day confess. A name that has no parallel in my vocabulary or yours. A name I whispered into the ears of my infant daughters as I rocked them and sang lullabies of His love. A name by which I've made every single prayerful petition of my life. A name that has meant my absolute salvation, not only from eternal destruction, but from myself. A name with power like no other name. *Jesus.*

What a beautiful name. I love to watch how it falls off the lips of those who love Him. I shudder as it falls off the lips of those who don't. *Jesus*. It has been the most important and most consistent word in my life. Dearer today than yesterday. Inexpressibly precious to me personally, so I am at a loss to comprehend what the name means universally.

Jesus. The Greek spelling is *Iesous*, transliterated from the Hebrew *Yeshu'a* (Joshua). Keep in mind that Christ's earthly family spoke a Semitic language closely related to Hebrew (called Aramaic), so He would have been called Yeshu'a. One of the things I like best is that it was a common name. After all, Jesus came to seek and to save common people like me. Most pointedly, the name Jesus means "Savior." Others may have shared the name, but no one else would ever share the role. We have much to learn about Jesus, the Savior. I can hardly wait!

What do you hope to experience at Jesus' feet as we worship Him together over the following days? What are you bringing that needs healing? What emptiness or brokenness needs mending? What do you want to say to Him at the outset of this journey? I hope to experience more about His love and how He never gives up. I am bringing things to God that are hard to put down on paper. I also want Him to fill the void of lonliness. I want Jesus to be my one and all.

PRAYING GOD'S WORD TODAY

O Lord, from ancient times You told Your people, "The virgin will conceive, have a son, and name him Immanuel" (Isa. 7:14), proving again the validity and consistency of Your Word. How I marvel at Your wisdom, Your truth, and Your eternal purposes, marveling even more that You choose to include one like me in Your plans and Your perfect will.

Lord God, Thank you for sending your Son Jesus. I want to learn so much about you and be guided in Your wisdom. Help me to listen to You and to follow You. Help me to also be a better bearer of Your name. Jesus I love you.

DAY 2

How Can This Be?

Before You Begin
Read Luke 1:34–38

Stop and Consider
Mary asked the angel, "How can this be,
since I have not been intimate with a man?" (v. 34).

When was the last time you read a verse of Scripture, or sensed a nudging of God in your spirit, and asked yourself, "How can this be?" _____

_____

_____

What would life be like without these kind of divine mysteries and impossibilities? What would we do if God never called us to greater things, to things that were more His size?

I think life would be easy and dull. We would have nothing to live for or strive for.

Luke 1:27 tells us that when the angel Gabriel appeared to Mary to announce that she would bear the Son of God, she was a virgin "pledged to be married to a man named Joseph." Actually, their betrothal compares more to our idea of *marriage* than engagement. The difference was the matter of physical intimacy, but the relationship was legally binding. Betrothal began with a contract drawn up by the parents or by a friend of the groom. Then at a meeting between the two families, in the presence of witnesses, the groom would present the bride with jewelry. The groom would announce his intentions to firmly observe the contract. Then he would sip from a cup of wine and offer the cup to the bride. If she sipped from the same cup, she was in effect entering covenant with him.

The next step was the payment of the *mohar*, or dowry, by the groom. This occurred at a ceremony, ordinarily involving a priest. Other traditions were also practiced, but these were the most basic and consistent. By the time a couple reached this step, their betrothal was binding, though a marriage ceremony and physical intimacy had not yet taken place. An actual divorce would be necessary to break the covenant. Furthermore, if the prospective groom died, the bride-to-be was considered a widow.

Betrothal traditionally occurred soon after the onset of adolescence, so it is probably accurate to imagine Mary around age thirteen at the time of the announcement. Remember, in that culture a thirteen or fourteen-year-old was commonly preparing for marriage.

Mary's question, then, was a quite obvious one: She asked, "How will this be . . . since I am a virgin?" (v. 34).

Gabriel met Mary's question with a beautifully expressive response. "The Holy Spirit will come upon you, and the power of the Most High will overshadow you." The Greek word for "come upon" is *eperchomai*, meaning "to . . . arrive, invade . . . resting upon and operating in a person." Only one woman in all of humanity would be chosen to bear the Son of God, yet each one of us who are believers have been invaded by Jesus Christ through His Holy Spirit (see Rom. 8:9). He has been invading the closets, the attic, and

the basement of my life ever since I accepted Him. How I praise God for the most glorious invasion of privacy that ever graced a human life!

I wonder if Mary knew when He arrived in her womb. Brothers in the faith might be appalled that I would ask such a question, but female minds were created to think intimate, personal thoughts like these! I have at least a hundred questions to ask Mary in heaven.

No doubt Mary would have some interesting stories to tell. Part of the fun of heaven will be hearing spiritual giants tell the details of the old, old stories. Mary certainly wouldn't have thought of herself as a spiritual giant, would she? I would love to know the exact moment this young adolescent absorbed the news that she would carry and deliver God's Son.

Gabriel ultimately wrapped up the story of the divine conception with one profound statement: "So the holy one to be born will be called the Son of God" (v. 35). The term *holy one* has never been more perfectly and profoundly applied than in Gabriel's statement concerning the Son of God.

Could a teenager have fathomed that she was to give birth to the Son who was the radiance of God's glory and the exact representation of His being? (Heb. 1:3). Perhaps Mary's age was on her side. When my two daughters were teenagers, and when they would tell me something, I always had more questions than they had answers. I'd say, "Did you ask this question?" to which they'd invariably say, "No, ma'am. Never even occurred to me." I wanted to know every detail. They were too young to realize any were missing!

Mary only asked the one question. When all was said and done, her solitary reply was: "I am the Lord's servant. . . . May it be to me as you have said" (v. 38). The Greek word for slave or servant is *doule*, which is the feminine equivalent to *doulos*, a male bondservant.

Praise God for the most glorious invasion of privacy ever to grace a human life—and that He has been invading my life ever since I accepted Him.

In essence, Mary was saying, "Lord, I am Your handmaid. Whatever You want, I want." Total submission. No other questions.

We might be tempted to think: *Easy for her to say! Her news was good! Who wouldn't want to be in her shoes? Submitting isn't hard when the news is good!* Oh, yes, the news was good. The best. But the news was also hard. When the winds of heaven converge with the winds of earth, lightning is bound to strike. Seems to me that Gabriel left just in time for Mary to tell her mother. I have a feeling Nazareth was about to hear and experience a little thunder.

Think of a time when you sensed the power of God "come upon you" in a moment of crisis, or worship, or perhaps on an otherwise ordinary day. What was it like, and why do you think He chooses when and how to reveal His presence so tangibly? I had gone to TTU to visit the campus with some kids from my youth group. We were sitting in chapel and one of the students was giving a testimony. During that time God "came upon me" and told me this was where He wanted me to go to college. It was an amazing feeling of peace. God chooses the right moments, when we are in His submission.

Praying God's Word Today

Lord, You have the authority to enable those of every people, nation, and language to serve You. Your dominion is an everlasting dominion that will not pass away, and Your kingdom is one that will not be destroyed (Dan. 7:14). In Your hands and by Your power, You can do through me whatever You desire. May I believe this in ever greater measure.

Lord, Thank you for reveling your presence to me in times of decisions and trials. Those moments bring me closer to you and give me the peace I need. Also during the times of worship where my heart is directed on you. Those are the best feelings. Lord, I ask that you work through me in whatever way you want. Show me if getting a degree in Library of Science is your will. Show me your presence.

DAY 3

Kindred Hearts

BEFORE YOU BEGIN
Read Luke 1:39–44

STOP AND CONSIDER
When Elizabeth heard Mary's greeting, the baby leaped inside her,
and Elizabeth was filled with the Holy Spirit (v. 41).

What are some of the greatest blessings (and greatest difficulties) of community?

Blessings – Fellowship,
difficulties – Dealing up hurt & grief & guilt

Second Corinthians 1 talks about the personal responsibility that comes along with "the comfort we ourselves receive from God" (v. 4). Why is it not enough just to receive it? Why do we need to share it around? _We need to share the_
Comfort of God so that Others can feel
it to. It may even lead Others to
Him.

Imagine that you are Mary, thirteen or fourteen years old, but in a very different culture. You awakened to the sun playing a silent reveille over the Galilean countryside. You dress in typical fashion, a simple tunic draped with a cloak. A sash wrapped around the waist allows you to walk without tripping over the long fabric. You are the virgin daughter of a Jewish father, so you have draped your veil over your head and crossed it over your shoulders for the duration of the day. You have never known another kind of dress, so you are completely accustomed to the weight and the constant adjusting of a six-foot-long, four-foot-wide veil. Beneath the veil, thick, dark hair frames a deep complexion and near-ebony eyes.

Without warning, a messenger from God appears and announces that you have been chosen among women to bear the Son of God. You can hardly believe, yet you dare not doubt. As suddenly as the angel appeared, he vanishes. You are flooded with emotions.

What do you imagine you would be thinking and feeling right now? What in the world does a young woman do after receiving such life-altering news?

Often God allows the space between the lines of His Word to capture our imaginations and prompt us to wonder. Not this time. He told us exactly what Mary did next.

Remember Gabriel's declaration. The most revolutionary news since Eden's fall: "the Savior is on His way." Announcing the soon-coming Messiah, he offered the stunned adolescent an almost out-of-place slice of information. By the way, "Elizabeth your relative is going to have a child in her old age, and she . . . is in her sixth month" (v. 36).

How like God! In the middle of news with universal consequences, He recognized the personal consequences to one girl.

For years the scene of Mary running to Elizabeth has tendered my heart. I'd like to share my thoughts on this moment from my first book, *Things Pondered: From the Heart of a Lesser Woman*. These words were never meant to provide doctrinal exegesis, but to invite us to the momentary wonder of being a woman:

"How tender the God who shared with her through an angel that someone nearby could relate. The two women had one important predicament in common—questionable pregnancies, sure to stir up some talk. Elizabeth hadn't been out of the house in months. It makes you wonder why. As happy as she was, it must have been strange not to blame her sagging figure and bumpy thighs on the baby. And to think she was forced to borrow maternity clothes from her friends' granddaughters. But maybe Elizabeth and Mary were too busy talking between themselves to pay much attention. Can you imagine their conversation over tea? One too old, the other too young. One married to an old priest, the other promised to a young carpenter. One heavy with child, the other with no physical evidence to fuel her faith. But God had graciously given them one another with a bond to braid their lives forever.

> In the middle of news with universal consequences, God recognized the personal consequences to one girl.

"Women are like that, aren't they? We long to find someone who has been where we've been, who shares our fragile places, who sees our sunsets with the same shades of blue."[1]

Elizabeth lived fifty to seventy miles from Nazareth. Mary had no small trip ahead of her and no small amount of time to replay the recent events. She probably joined others making the trip, but we have no reason to assume anyone traveled with her. Can you imagine how different she was already beginning to feel? How did it feel to finally enter the village Zechariah and Elizabeth called home? What do you imagine was going through Mary's mind as she passed village merchants and mothers with children?

Finally, Mary entered Zechariah's home and greeted Elizabeth. Mary's words of salutation may have been common, but Elizabeth's reaction was far from common. The infant John jumped within his mother's womb, and Elizabeth was suddenly "filled with the Holy

Spirit" (v. 41). Elizabeth proclaimed Mary and her child "blessed" and asked a glorious question: "Why am I so favored, that the mother of my Lord should come to me?" (v. 43).

Mary and Elizabeth shared not only tender similarities but also vital differences. Elizabeth pointed out the most profound difference: she was expecting her son; Mary was expecting her Lord. The concepts seem almost unfathomable even with the complete revelation of the Word. Don't miss the riches that follow Elizabeth's inspiring question. She went on to announce: "As soon as the sound of your greeting reached my ears, the baby in my womb leaped for joy. Blessed is she who has believed that what the Lord has said to her will be accomplished!" (Luke 1:44–45).

Has God ever provided you someone to share your joy in the impossible or to understand the peculiar place you find yourself in? Describe how it impacted you. And determine how you will be used of God to be that person for someone else, when the need arises. _____

God has brought to me many people in which I can talk to. Most of them have not gone through the same thing I have, but they can relate. It helps me to know someone else has gone through something close and they show me how God has worked in that situation.

PRAYING GOD'S WORD TODAY

Father of mercies, God of all comfort, thank You for comforting us in our affliction, not merely that we might sense Your renewal and refreshment, but also that we may be able to comfort those who are in any kind of affliction, through the comfort we ourselves have received from You (2 Cor. 1:3–4). Thank You for making us an instrument of Your mercy and healing to others. Heavenly Father, thank You for be the Comforter. I have needed Your loving arms to wrap around me and You have always been there. As I continue through some of these afflictions, help me to see Your outstretched arms waiting for me. Also, let me show Your comfort to Others who are in need.

DAY 4

Mary's Song

BEFORE YOU BEGIN

Read Luke 1:46–55

STOP AND CONSIDER

The Mighty One has done great things for me, and His name is holy (v. 49).

We are prone to dwell on our own weaknesses and shortcomings. But if someone were to really look inside, what evidence of God's work would they see in you? (It's not boastful to praise Him for what He does!) *I can sing, I'm a good listener, caring*

If you were to write a song today, what words and phrases would you want to employ?

God is great and wonderful.
There is joy in serving the Lord.
Praise Him for all He has done.

Mary's wonderful words from her Magnificat offer us an opportunity to catch a glimpse of several facts about her:

Her excitement. Mary had probably been too scared to celebrate before, but Elizabeth's confirmation of God's miraculous work set her free! How do I know? Behold verse 47: "My spirit rejoices in God my Savior." The original word for "rejoices" is *agalliao*, meaning "to exult, leap for joy, to show one's joy by leaping and skipping denoting excessive or ecstatic joy and delight. Often spoken of rejoicing with song and dance." Whether or not young Mary began physically jumping up and down with joy and excitement, her insides certainly did! I am totally blessed by the thought. Nothing is more appropriate than getting excited when God does something in our lives. I think He loves it!

Her love of Scripture. Mary's song reflects twelve different Old Testament passages. She didn't just hear the Word; she held it to her heart and pondered it. Scripture draws a picture of a reflective young woman with an unusual heart for God. A young Hebrew girl believed nothing to be as important as motherhood. I believe she must have recalled a favorite Old Testament story when she received the news. Mary sang praises to God just as Hannah had done over the birth of Samuel.

Her humility. Her statement that "all generations will call me blessed" (v. 48) was not voiced in pride but from shock. Mary reminds me of David, who said: "Who am I, O Sovereign LORD, and what is my family, that you have brought me this far? . . . Is this your usual way of dealing with man, O Sovereign LORD?" (2 Sam. 7:18–19). In a way, the answer to his question is yes. God seems to love little more than stunning the humble with His awesome intervention.

Her experience. Please don't lose the wonder of it. Marvel with me at the fact that she was plain, simple, and extraordinarily ordinary. I always felt the same way growing up. Still do, deep down inside. That's part of the beauty of God choosing someone like you and me to know Him and serve Him. May we never get over it.

PRAYING GOD'S WORD TODAY

Like Mary, Lord, my heart rejoices in You today. My mouth boasts over my enemies—those many, many strongholds that have held me prisoner far too long—even Satan himself, who has been rendered defeated by Your great salvation. There is no one holy like You, Lord. In fact, there is no one besides You! There is no rock like our God! (1 Sam. 2:1–2).

Lord, You are wonderful and praise you. Thank You for creating the world. Your creations are outstanding. You are a blessing. Thank You for all you have done in my life and for never giving up on me. I pray that I will continue to follow Your will for my life.

DAY 5

*A Good Time
to Celebrate*

Before You Begin

Read Luke 2:1–7

Stop and Consider

In those days a decree went out from Caesar Augustus

that the whole empire should be registered (v. 1).

What do you love most about celebrating the birth of Christ? *Knowing that He came as a baby to grow up and save the world from sin*

What would you say to those who think this holiday is somewhat sacrilegious, that mingling something so sacred with something so increasingly secular cheapens our worship? *I would agree with them. People tend to focus on the material reasons for Christmas and they put Christ in Christmas just because they have to.*

I have heard the questions thousands of times: Why do we celebrate Christmas on December 25? How do we know when the birth of Christ took place? Why celebrate Christmas at a time originally set for ancient pagan celebrations?

The Scrooges are right; we don't know when Christ was born. But I happen to think His is a birth worthy of celebrating at some time of year. After all, God didn't just tolerate celebrations and festivals commemorating His faithfulness—He commanded them! His idea! Some were solemn; others were for the pure purpose of rejoicing before the Lord.

On one such occasion Nehemiah said, "Go and enjoy choice food and sweet drinks, and send some to those who have nothing prepared. This day is sacred to our Lord. Do not grieve, for the joy of the Lord is your strength" (Neh. 8:10). The Book of Esther also speaks of an annual day set aside for "joy and feasting . . . a day for giving presents to each other" (Esther 9:19). The most concentrated list of Old Testament feasts appears in Leviticus 23. The chapter describes seven different feasts. In verse 5 we read, "The LORD's Passover begins at twilight on the fourteenth day of the first month."

The first month falls, according to the new moon, over the last half of March and the first half of April. The timing has significance to all of us who have carried children in our wombs. In the Jewish calendar, the fourteenth day of the first month is called the day of conception. If our God of perfect planning and gloriously significant order happened to overshadow Mary on the fourteenth day of the first month of His calendar, our Savior would have been born toward the end of our December. We have absolutely no way of knowing whether or not He did, but I would not be the least bit surprised for God to have sparked His Son's human life on one Passover and ended it on another.

No, I don't believe in Easter bunnies, and I don't have much of an opinion on Santa Clauses, but I'm a hopeless romantic when it comes to celebrating Christmas, the birth of my Savior. Until a further "Hear ye! Hear ye!" comes from heaven, December 25 works mighty fine for me.

PRAYING GOD'S WORD TODAY

O Lord, may we never lack desire to speak of Your glorious splendor and Your wonderful works, declaring Your greatness from one generation to the next. May we proclaim and celebrate the power of Your awe-inspiring works, giving testimony of Your great goodness and joyfully singing of Your righteousness (Ps. 145:5–7).

Precious Savior, Thank You
for sending us Your Son.
I am not worthy to receive
His love, but He gives it to me
Anyway. Lord, I want to
praise You and worship You
for Your great and mighty works.
and all the splendor You
created. You gave them to us
And I pray we use all to Your
glory.

DAY 6

Perfect Timing

BEFORE YOU BEGIN
Read Galatians 4:3–7

STOP AND CONSIDER

But when the completion of the time came, God sent His Son, born of a woman,
born under the law, to redeem those under the law (vv. 4–5).

What has God shown you in your own life about His timing . . . His perfect timing?

> That when it's His timing, every
> thing works out and I'm happy
> or full of joy.

How does this sovereign power of God strike you? Does it leave you feeling confined and
hemmed in? Or does it make you feel totally secure and at rest in His eternal purposes?

> Sometimes it just irks me because I
> want things to happen now. Other times
> I feel at peace knowing that it will
> be perfect in His time.

God purposed that His Son would come out of Nazareth but be born in Bethlehem. So He caused a census to require everyone in the Roman world to return to the place of his or her family's origin. Probably the timing was too close to the birth of the child for Joseph to leave Mary behind. One commentary tenderly suggested that Joseph may not have wanted Mary left behind and subjected to gossip.

Bethlehem is about five miles south of Jerusalem, quite a distance from Nazareth, with chains of hills and mountains in between. Theirs was no easy trip. Women could be tempted to picket the New International Version for leaving out one little detail that had a profound influence on Mary's trip: "Mary . . . being great with child" (Luke 2:5 KJV). We have to appreciate the fact that the verb tense indicates a continuous action. We might say she was getting greater by the minute.

I certainly remember feeling that way. I'll never forget catching a glimpse of myself, great with child, in the distorted reflection of the stainless-steel faucet on the tub. My stomach looked huge, and my head and arms appeared like nubs. From then on I took showers. Taking "great with child" on the road is no easy task.

Whether or not Mary and Joseph planned Christ's birth this way, God certainly did. One of my favorite phrases in the birth narrative is humbly tucked in Luke 2:6: "While they were there, the time came for the baby to be born." The time. The time toward which all "time" had been ticking since the kingdom clock struck one.

These words refer to the most important segment of time since the first tick of the clock. The second hand circled tens of thousands of times for thousands of years, then finally, miraculously, majestically—the time came. God's voice broke through the barrier of the natural realm through the cries of an infant, startled by life on the outside. The Son of God had come to earth, wrapped in a tiny cloak of human flesh. "She wrapped him in cloths and placed him in a manger, because there was no room for them in the inn" (v. 7).

PRAYING GOD'S WORD TODAY

Father God, You have brought all things together in Christ—things both in heaven and on earth. In Him, You have made us Your inheritance, predestined according to Your eternal purpose—You who work out everything in agreement with Your will. Therefore, we who have put our hope in Jesus our Messiah praise His glorious name (Eph. 1:10–12). Obedient to Your call, He has met us in our deepest need . . . just when we needed Him most.

Lord Jesus, one thing I have learned is that Your timing is perfect. But, one thing I need to work on is waiting for Your timing. I have had my hopes up planning for something to come and it hasn't because I was going before Your time. Help to put more faith in You and truly trust in Your timing.

DAY 7

Heaven Came Down

BEFORE YOU BEGIN
Read Luke 2:8–14

STOP AND CONSIDER

The angel said to them, "Don't be afraid, for look, I proclaim to you
good news of great joy that will be for all people" (v. 10).

What is your attitude toward common, ordinary, rough-around-the-edges people? How
do you approach them, see them, respond to them? *Most of the time
I see them as being just like me
and approach them as someone
would me.*

What would be different or would have to change about God's "good news" if it wasn't
intended for "all people"? *It would be "good news"
if it wasn't intended for "all people."
It would be associated with that
group and would mean anything to
other people.*

Luke 2 identifies the first persons to receive the glorious announcement of Christ's birth. Why do you think God first proclaimed the good news to a motley crew of sheepherders? He seems to enjoy revealing Himself to common people rather than to those who feel most worthy. He often uses the foolish things of this world to confound the wise (see 1 Cor. 1:28). Maybe God had a soft place in His heart for the shepherds watching over their flocks.

Don't miss the fact that the announcement came to the shepherds while they were watching over their flocks "at night" (v. 8). Sometimes in the contrast of the night, we can best see the glory of God. Verse 9 tells us that "the glory of the Lord shone around them." Notice the Scripture does not say that the glory of the Lord shone around the angel but around the shepherds. As you picture the scene, keep in mind that only one angel, an angel of the Lord, appeared to them first. The other heavenly hosts did not join the scene until after the birth announcement. Most definitely, the glory shone around the shepherds.

Try to imagine for a moment what happened. How do you think the glory of the Lord looked around the shepherds? We don't know for sure; I'm just asking you to picture it in your mind right now.

I am convinced that God wants us to get involved in our Scripture reading. Using our imaginations and picturing the events as eye-witnesses can make black ink on a white page spring into living color. No matter how the glory of God appeared, it scared the shepherds half to death. The words of the angel are so reminiscent of my Savior. Often He told those nearly slain by His glory not to be afraid.

Oh, how I love Him. The untouchable Hand of God reaching down to touch the fallen hand of man. "I bring you good news of great joy that will be for all the people" (v. 10). I am convinced our witness would be far more effective if we brought our good news with great joy.

PRAYING GOD'S WORD TODAY

How I thank You, Lord Jesus, that Your good news is for all people, that we who were once alienated and hostile toward You because of our evil actions have now been reconciled through Your death. Even more, we who deserved death and shame have been presented before You holy, faultless, and blameless (Col. 1:21–22). May I live to worship You for such amazing grace, and live to tell of its wonders to others. _____

Jesus, thank you that your
Good news is for all people. Thats
whats so amazing about you. You
want all people to know you
and know your love. Help me to
tell others about you and show
your glorious and Magnificent
Love and tell your Good news.

DAY 8

A Night of Nights

Before You Begin
Read Luke 2:15–20

Stop and Consider
But Mary was treasuring up all these things in her heart and meditating on them (v. 19).

What would have to change in your life for you to experience more times of "treasuring" your blessings, of "meditating" on the goodness and greatness of God? *I would have to stop watching TV and playing computer games.*

If you did, what do you think would be the result of it? How would it benefit you? How would it alter your perspectives? *I would become closer to God because I would have more time to spend with Him.*

How do you suppose Mary felt on the night of nights after Jesus had been born? The following are just some thoughts that God gave me as I tried to imagine what it would have been like over those next couple of hours. But I want to be very clear here: this is strictly fiction. I just invite you to imagine with me what Mary's first moments might have been like as a mother:

Her body lay sapped of strength, her eyes were heavily closed, but her mind refused to give way to rest. She ached for her mother. She wondered if she yet believed her. She heard the labored breathing of the man sleeping a few feet from her. Only months before he was little more than a stranger to her. She knew only what she had been told and what she could read in occasional shy glances. She had been told he was a good man. Over the last few days, she found out he was far more than a good man. No man, no matter how kind, could have done what he had done. She wondered how long it had been since he'd really rested.

A calf, only a few days old, awakened hungry and could not find its mother. The stir awakened the baby who also squirmed to find His mother. Scarcely before she could move her tender frame toward the manger, He began to wail! She scooped Him in her arms, her long hair draping His face, and she quietly slipped out of the gate. She gingerly sat down and leaned against the outside of the stable, propped the baby on her small lap, and taking a strip of linen and tying back her hair, she began to stare into His tiny face. She had not yet seen Him in the light. She had never seen the moon so bright. The night was nearly as light as the day. Only hours old, His chin quivered, not from the cold, but from the sudden exposure of birth. His eyes were shaped like almonds and were as black as the deepest well. She held Him tightly and quietly hummed a song she'd learned as a child. She had been so frightened of this moment, so sure she would not know what to do. She had never held an infant so small, and He was God, wrapped in soft, infant flesh, with bones so fragile she felt like He could break. She had pictured this moment so many times. What would the Son of the Spirit look like? She never expected Him to look so normal, so common.

Must have been the part He inherited from His mother. She was so sure she'd feel terribly awkward. So afraid she'd drop Him—the Messiah—and God would be awfully sorry He had given Him to her! Instead, every fear, every doubt, every inadequacy was momentarily caught up in the indescribable rapture of a mother's affection.

She remembered asking Elizabeth things she dared not ask her father and mother. Once when they were walking together at the end of the day, the wind blew her cousin's robes against her, and like a curious teenager, Mary tried her hardest to catch a good glimpse of Elizabeth's rounded middle. At the time she herself had no physical evidence that God's promise was true. But she had enough faith to ask endless questions. What am I to do when He comes? Her cousin's reply would remain etched upon Mary's heart long after He had saved the world. He will tell you what He needs from you. Beyond what He needs, all He wants is for you to embrace Him and talk to Him.

> "Sweet baby boy. Do You know who Your Daddy is? Do You know Your name? Do You know why You're here? Will You love me too?"

She looked back into His delicate face and watched Him closely as He seemed to stare deeply into the moonlit sky. And she began to talk. "Sweet baby boy. Do You know who Your Daddy is? Do You know Your name? Do You know why You're here? What do You see when You look out there? Can You see the stars? Do You remember their names? Do You think I'll do OK? Will You love me too?" A tear dropped from her chin to His. He yawned and made such a funny expression she grinned, wiping her face on the yellowed rags she'd draped around Him. The fussing calf had obviously found its mother. Not a sound was coming from inside the stable. The earth stilled. The infant slept. She held the babe next to her face, and for just a moment, all the world was silent to the breath of God.

She closed her eyes and listened, stealing time like a hidden metronome, as high and as wide as she dared to think, but she still could not begin to comprehend. She, a common child of the most humble means who had never read the Scriptures for herself, was embracing the incarnate Word. The fullness of the Godhead rested in her inexperienced arms, sleeping to the rhythm of her heart. This time she hummed a song she did not know, a song being sung by the choir of angels hovering over her head but hidden from her carnal senses. The deafening hallelujahs of the heavenly hosts were silent to mortal ears except through the sounds of a young woman's voice who had unknowingly given human notes to a holy score. The glory of God filled the earth. Heaven hammered a bridge, but one young woman sat completely unaware of all that swelled the atmosphere around her. The tiny baby boy had robbed her heart. "So, this is how it feels to be a mother," she mused.

She crept back into the stable, wrapped Him in swaddling clothes and laid Him in the manger. Just down the path, the sun peeked gently over the roof of an inn full of barren souls who had made Him no room.

What have you sensed in your heart as you've imagined these things with me? What are the real-life qualities of Christ that most surprise you to think of them? _I sensed peace and love. The qualities that most surprise me are the characteristics of a baby. Knowing that God needed someone to take care of Him._

Praying God's Word Today

I will sing to You, Lord, all my life, trusting that my meditation will always be pleasing to You (Ps. 104:33–34). May the words of my mouth and the meditation of my heart be acceptable to You, O Lord, my rock and my redeemer (Ps. 19:14).

Jesus, I need to meditate more on You and focus more on You. I want to praise You and proclaim Your Holiness. I need to make the time to spend with You and not focus on the worldly things.

DAY 9

Covenant and
Redemption

BEFORE YOU BEGIN
Read Luke 2:21–24

STOP AND CONSIDER
When the days of their purification according to the law of Moses were finished,
they brought Him up to Jerusalem to present Him to the Lord (v. 22).

What is the difference between being obedient to custom—in being merely traditional—
and being faithful to do what God has commanded? *Being Obedient*
to customs means your doing it because thats
whats suppose to be done. Being faithful to
what God has commanded means You
want to do it.

Which religious customs and disciplines carry the most meaning for you—not just in their
warm feelings of nostalgia but in their true spiritual significance? *Praising*
and worshiping God through song. Also
Communion has become more meaningful
to me.

Jesus' parents had Him circumcised on the eighth day of His young life. Then they presented Him at the temple and offered the sacrifices required of new parents. Each of the steps Mary and Joseph took after Christ's birth was typical of devout Jewish parents. What made these events atypical is that their infant would ultimately fulfill the prophetic representation of each of these rituals. Let's take a brief look at all three rites: circumcision, redemption, and purification.

The Rite of Circumcision. We read about circumcision in Genesis 17:1–14. It was so important that verse 11 says it would serve as "a sign of the covenant between me and you." Verse 14 says an uncircumcised male "will be cut off from his people; he has broken my covenant." The rite of circumcision was God's way of requiring the Jewish people to become physically different because of their relationship to Him.

A careful reading of Colossians 2:9–15 sheds light on how the infant Jesus would later be used to fulfill a different kind of circumcision in believers. Verse 11 says: "In him you were also circumcised, in the putting off of the sinful nature." If you have walked with Jesus for any time, you can point to ways in which our spiritual circumcision results in proof that we are different than the persons we originally were.

When the infant Jesus was circumcised at eight days of age, I'm not sure His parents could fathom that He was the physical manifestation of the covenant God had made thousands of years earlier. Second Corinthians 1:20 says, "No matter how many promises God has made, they are 'Yes' in Christ." The infant that Joseph held during Jesus' circumcision was the very Yes of God to the promise of the covenant being symbolized.

The Rite of Redemption. In Luke 2:22–24 two distinct rites were observed by Mary and Joseph. Before we research them, please note that a segment of time has passed between the circumcision and the presentation. According to Leviticus 12:1–8 a woman was to wait thirty-three days after the circumcision before presenting a son at the temple. Exodus 13 tells us the reason why every firstborn male was to be redeemed. The redemption was a reminder that "the LORD brought us out of Egypt with his mighty hand" (v. 16).

Mary and Joseph went to Jerusalem in obedience to this command. Like all devout Jewish parents, they presented their infant to the Lord to depict sacrifice and redemption. When Jewish parents presented their firstborn son to the Lord, they were symbolizing the act of giving him up by saying, "He is Yours and we give him back to You." Then they would immediately redeem him or, in effect, buy him back.

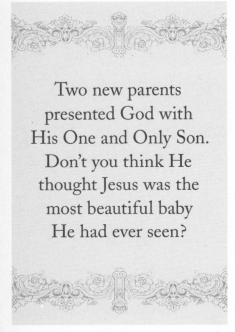

Two new parents presented God with His One and Only Son. Don't you think He thought Jesus was the most beautiful baby He had ever seen?

Few teachings are more important and consistent in God's Word than the doctrine of redemption. The Hebrew word is *padhah*, meaning "to redeem by paying a price." The New Testament tells us Christ came to fulfill for us the very rite Mary and Joseph observed as they presented the Christ child to the Lord.

Ephesians 1:7 says, "In him we have redemption through his blood, the forgiveness of sins, in accordance with the riches of God's grace." Consider this verse from the apostle Paul's Jewish perspective. He drew a parallel to our entrance into the family of God. Since most of us are Gentiles, we are considered the "adopted ones" in God's family. What was true in a tangible sense after the birth of a Jewish son is true of us in a spiritual sense after our rebirth as "sons" of God. We all must be redeemed. The wonderful picture for us, however, is that we are not bought from God by our natural parents. Rather, Christ buys us from our natural parentage, which is sinful flesh, to give us to His Father. If the concept is too confusing, just celebrate that Christ has redeemed you!

The Rite of Purification. The rite of redemption was distinct from the rite of purification. This purification is described in Leviticus 12:1–8. The prescribed sacrifice included a lamb, but the law made provision for impoverished parents. Verse 8 says, "If she cannot afford a lamb, she is to bring two doves or two young pigeons." Luke told us that Jesus' parents offered the poverty version of the sacrifice.

Have you ever considered what Christ's earthly poverty has to do with us? Second Corinthians 8:9 proclaims that "though he was rich, yet for your sakes he became poor, so that you through his poverty might become rich."

Mary and Joseph offered the least sacrifice permitted by Jewish law for the rite of purification. How fitting that they held in their arms the greatest sacrifice a holy God could ever make for their eternal purification. Titus 2:14 tells us that Jesus Christ "gave himself for us to redeem us from all wickedness and to purify for himself a people that are his very own."

The Word made flesh first entered the temple wrapped in a baby blanket. His earthly parents lifted Him to His Father and, in essence, purchased Him from heaven—for a while—for a lost world. One day that baby would buy them from earth for the glory of heaven. Wow.

What does your heart say to you as you witness the perfection and continuity of God's Word in Christ—the perfect joining of Old Testament promise and New Testament fulfillment?

God's Word is true.

Praying God's Word Today

I'm grateful, Lord, that in obedience, there is life—that in the consistent honoring of Your Word, You cause our relationship to grow and deepen. Your precepts are right, making the heart glad. Your commandments are radiant, making the eyes light up. Your ordinances are reliable and altogether righteous (Ps. 19:8–9). Everything about You is consistency, stability, and truth. Dear Lord, Thank You for sending Your Son to be my redemption. I do not deserve this, but because of Your love, You have given it to me. Lord, I want to follow in all Your ways. Guide me in the months to come to make the right decisions about the future. I cannot do this alone.

DAY 10

Listening, Answering

Before You Begin
Read Luke 2:41–47

Stop and Consider

After three days, they found Him in the temple complex sitting among
the teachers, listening to them and asking them questions . . . and all those who
heard Him were astounded at His understanding and His answers (vv. 46–47).

What are some of the questions you have for Him right now? And how assured are you
that He is listening? _Right now I have tons of_
questions about the future and I know
He is listening to every single one.

What do you think it will require for you to be receptive to "His understanding and His
answers"? _It will require submission_
to Him.

I had the joy of raising my children alongside my best friend of twenty-plus years. Numerous times we thought one of our children was with the other, only to find the child in the dog bowl or splashing in the toilet. We feel fortunate we didn't leave any of them while on a vacation somewhere.

I'm not sure anything prompts emotions like finding a lost child. Fear surges through your heart during the search. Relief floods over you when you find the child safe. Then if the child discounts parental concern, emotions surge to vengeance!

Yet even though I feel compassion concerning Mary's and Joseph's fear, I love what they found their son doing on the third day of their search—sitting in the temple, conversing with the teachers:

"Listening." I'm so thankful Christ not only speaks, He also listens. We don't know if God allowed the twelve-year-old Christ to exercise His full omniscience or to unleash just enough wisdom to astound His listeners. But I love the fact that Christ still listens—not just to learn, since He knows all things. Rather, He allows us to pour out our hearts because He loves us and wants to hear us.

"Asking them questions." Contrary to popular belief, faith is not the avoidance of questions. Our faith grows when we seek answers, and we find many between Genesis 1:1 and Revelation 22:21. We may hear a gentle, "Because I said so," to those questions God chooses not to answer, but I don't believe our heavenly Father is offended by questions. Part of Christlikeness is learning to listen and ask appropriate questions, even of those you respect in the faith.

"His answers." As we go along in this devotional journey, we will see several examples of Him posing a question only He could answer. Christ certainly uses that teaching method with me. Sometimes He'll cause me to dig through Scripture for a question He seemed to initiate. Other times the question may come as a personalized whisper in my heart. Then as He reveals my insecurities and fleshly defense mechanisms, He gives me new understanding. He answers me, so that I don't have to live off my own answers.

PRAYING GOD'S WORD TODAY

O Lord Jesus, just as during Your earthly life You offered prayers and appeals to the Father with loud cries and tears—and were heard because of Your reverence and submission (Heb. 5:7)—I pray that I too would come before You in perfect trust, knowing that You always live to intercede for us (Heb. 7:25). Jesus, Thank You so much for listening to me. I know I tend to prattle on and on, but You still listen. Thank You also for listening to my questions. I know I'm not sure about the near future, but I know You will give to the best answers.

DAY 11

What It's All About

Before You Begin

Read Luke 2:48–50

Stop and Consider

"Why were you searching for Me?" He asked them.

"Didn't you know that I had to be in My Father's house?" (v. 49).

When was the last time you received an answer from the Lord that seemed this far above your ability to understand it? *Just a couple of weeks ago when I asked Him about my future and He puts me back in the classroom.*

What do you do with answers from His Word that either seem not to make sense or seem impossible to emulate? *I just go with it and ask God for His guidance and understanding.*

Mary, understandably hurt that Jesus had chosen to hang back in Jerusalem and leave them to worry about His safety, asked Him a question in verse 48: "Son, why have you treated us like this?" Christ's response in verse 49 suggests He was as mystified that they'd expect to find Him anywhere else as they were mystified to find Him there: "Didn't you know I had to be in my Father's house?"

The words "had to" come from the Greek word *dei*, meaning something that is "inevitable in the nature of things." Likely this word has never been used more literally. After all, the Father and the Son had the same nature. Christ was drawn to God, not as a devout believer, but as an overpowering magnet—as two pieces of the same whole.

Still, the fact remains that Mary had asked a question, and Jesus had given an answer. But verse 50 tells us that she didn't understand the answer He supplied.

This remains part of our experience today. I believe we are always free to ask Jesus questions. And I believe He is always faithful to answer, even though his answer may not be speedy in coming. But even if it does come immediately, we may not *understand* the answer until later. Maybe much later.

In my opinion, Christ's response was quite interesting. I've searched every Greek translation I can find, and none of my resources have an original word that directly translates to "house" (NIV) or "business" (KJV) in verse 49. From what I can gather, a more precise translation of Christ's response might be: "Didn't you know that I had to be about my Father?"

That question implies the desire of my heart more than any other I can imagine. I just want to be about God. Not about ministry. Not about my own agenda. Not about writing Bible studies. Not about me at all. When all is said and done, I would give my life for people to be able to say, "She was just about God." That would be the ultimate legacy. "Not that I have already obtained all this . . . but I press on" (Phil. 3:12). May we live lives that would cause others to be surprised to find us any other place than to "be found in him" (Phil. 3:9).

Praying God's Word Today

Lord God, Your light has shone into my darkness, and has exchanged it for the light of the knowledge of Your glory in the face of Christ (2 Cor. 4:6). I pray that I will never be allured by the light of any other false attraction, but will ever find my joy in Your light, in Your life . . . in You. Lord, I want to be about God. I want Your light to shine through me. Help me to do better in the classroom. Help me to show Your love to these students. I want Your passion. I want to show these kids that You are all they need. Help me be a light to each child in my House

DAY 12

Picturing Jesus

BEFORE YOU BEGIN
Read Luke 2:39–40, 51–52

STOP AND CONSIDER
Jesus increased in wisdom and stature, and in favor with God and with people (v. 52).

What image do you think most people have of the man, Jesus of Nazareth. And why do think they perceive Him that way? He was a good, loving man.

In today's reading, I'll share some of the qualities I most like in people. What would be on your list if you were to make one? And which of them can you see Jesus possessing? Friendliness, caring, outgoing, thoughtfulness, Kindness, etc. I see Jesus possessing all.

Luke 2:52 appears brief and to the point but actually broadens dramatically our concept of Christ during those years when He went from boy to mature man.

Jesus grew in wisdom. The Greek word for "wisdom" is *sophia*. Consider two segments of the definition: (1) *Sophia* is skill in the affairs of life, practical wisdom, and wise management as shown in forming the best plans and selecting the best means, including the idea of sound judgment and good sense. (2) In respect to divine things, *sophia* is wisdom, knowledge, insight, deep understanding. So as you seek to formulate an impression of what Christ was like in His earthly form, please view Him as both completely practical and deeply spiritual. In fact, Christ came to show us that the deeply spiritual is very practical.

I encourage you to avoid imagining Christ as so deep you'd have to dig to find Him or so spiritual His head is in the clouds. He came bringing heaven to earth. In today's terms, He was a man who could preach an anointed sermon, then change a flat tire on the way home from church.

No wonder Christ became such a rare teacher! Believing people are starving for a wisdom that is both deeply spiritual and vastly practical. Christ embodied every dimension of wisdom in His earthly life, even before He officially began His public ministry.

Jesus grew in stature. This phrase tells us the obvious: Christ grew physically (and mentally) in the vigor and stature of a man. What is, of course, less obvious is what He grew to look like. God's Word lets us use our permanent markers only once as we try to imagine Christ's appearance, even though our solitary source happens to be one of my least favorite verses. God knows my heart and why I feel this way.

Isaiah 53:2 predicts about the coming Messiah: "He had no beauty or majesty to attract us to him, nothing in his appearance that we should desire him." I simply cannot imagine Christ not being beautiful, but I also believe beauty is in the eye of the beholder. All of us can think of people who are beautiful to us but whose faces might never be chosen for a magazine cover. Don't read more into Isaiah 53:2 than is there, however. The intent of the original terms is that He didn't have a magnificent, godlike physical appearance that

attracted people to Him. The descriptions don't necessarily imply that Christ was unattractive but that His looks were most likely ordinary.

Jesus grew in favor with God. Oh, how I love picturing the relationship Christ shared with His heavenly Father. I will limit my comments for now because I don't want to steal the joy of discovery as we search out dimensions of their relationship in the days to come.

> In today's terms, He was a man who could preach an anointed sermon, then change a flat tire on the way home from church.

For now, note what the word *favor* means. The Greek word is *charis*, which is often translated "grace" in the New Testament. *Charis* means "grace, particularly that which causes joy, pleasure, gratification, favor, acceptance." Jesus' growing in favor with God basically implies that their relationship became an increasing delight to both of them. Without a doubt, the relationship between God the Father and God the Son is totally unique. Indeed Jesus is the One and Only—the only begotten of the Father. And the relationship the two of them shared while Christ was earthbound is unparalleled.

Jesus grew in favor with men. As we attempt to formulate a picture of Christ's stature and personality, this description is extremely important. Isaiah 53:3 tells us that He was despised and rejected by men. But understand that He was not despised and rejected until He became a complete threat to the establishment. Actually, His popularity was the driving force behind Jesus' opponents' lust for His blood.

In Luke 2:52, God states Christ's favor with men, but throughout the Gospels He demonstrates it. Fishermen don't leave their nets to follow someone void of personality. People didn't just respect Him—they liked Him. The word *favor* is undeniably related to the word *favorite*. I don't believe we are stretching the text in the least to say that Christ was a favorite of many who knew Him.

Think for a few moments of the different characteristics of people who tend to capture your favor. Unless those characteristics are inconsistent with godliness, in all likelihood Christ possessed them. I can readily share a few of my favorite characteristics in people: godly, warm, and personable, at least somewhat demonstrative, knowledgeable in a specific area so I can learn from them, trustworthy, and funny! Although God's Word tells us that we are not to show favoritism, all of us have favorite characteristics we enjoy in people. You can safely assume that Christ possessed many of the dimensions you would favor most.

I simply want you to be reminded that He was real. His sandals flapped when He walked down the road. His hair was misshapen when He awakened. He had to brush the bread crumbs off His beard after He ate. The muscles in His arms flexed when He lifted His little brothers and sisters. He had hair on His arms and warmth in His palms. He was the Son of God and the Son of man. Fathom the unfathomable.

In what way is this exercise helpful to you? Or new to you? How does it alter (if at all) the picture you have of Jesus in your mind's eye? *This exercise just helps me see more of the physical human characteristics that Jesus had. I pictured Him more of a "Godly" appearance the a human one.*

Praying God's Word Today

How I long to grow with my brothers and sisters into the knowledge of Your Son, growing into a mature person with a stature measured by Christ's fullness—not tossed by the waves and blown around by every wind of teaching, but walking in the truth, growing in every way into Him who is the head—our Lord and Savior, Jesus Christ (Eph. 4:13–15).

Thank you Jesus for being
the way you were on earth.
It's hard to put into words What
I'm saying, but I know you
understand.
Thank you for never giving
up on me and always guiding
me. Help me to possess more
qualities that will glorify you.

DAY 13

Wearing
Our Transgressions

BEFORE YOU BEGIN
Read Matthew 3:1–6

STOP AND CONSIDER
They were baptized by him in the Jordan River as they confessed their sins (v. 6).

What's the purpose of confession and repentance after we've already been forgiven of our sins? Why does God still demand and expect it of us? *If we do not confess our sins, we can fall into to hands of Satan and fall away from God.*

In your times of repentance, what do you find the Lord doing in your heart? What does He achieve during these moments that never seem to happen at any other time? *I feel depressed and guilty. I feel God convicting me and showing me where I went wrong. This is when I fall at His feet and give my heart back to Him.*

We can almost picture John waist-deep in water with people streaming out to be baptized. They were confessing their sins, because they weren't being baptized unto salvation. John was baptizing them unto repentance, preparing them to encounter the Savior, the only One who could bring them salvation.

I believe they were quite specific confessing their sins. In all likelihood they were crying out these confessions, maybe even wailing them, weeping over their sins. Then came Christ. We know *He* was not coming to be baptized unto repentance. He was the spotless Lamb of God. Complete perfection. He was the only One who had no confessing to do that day in those waters. He came for John to baptize Him.

I just want you to get the picture here. I'm not trying to make a doctrinal statement or an interpretation of Scripture. I'm just asking you to see a picture. We know that God was baptizing His Son into ministry—the representation of the death, the burial, and the resurrection. But I also see something so precious in the fact that the people had confessed their sins standing in those same waters and then were baptized. Christ comes after they've made these confessions. He is baptized—drenched in the same waters where they had confessed their sins. I'm just talking symbolism here, but do you almost see Him wearing the sins they had confessed in those waters?

I love the practice of daily coming to the line with Christ and naming my sins. I don't practice a "Lord, forgive me for all of my sins." I don't see true biblical repentance in that. Repentance assumes we are naming the sin to acknowledge it. Then I like to discuss with God why it doesn't agree with His Word, why the sin isn't what He wants for me. That kind of repentance begins to get those precepts down into my soul.

I love Acts 3:19: "Repent, then, and turn to God, so that your sins may be wiped out, that times of refreshing may come from the Lord." Those of us who have already received Christ have been baptized into Him. Now daily confession is like refreshment to our souls. We come away from repentance cleansed. Ready to be filled. Ready to walk in the Spirit.

PRAYING GOD'S WORD TODAY

Lord, You have said, "It is I who sweep away your transgressions for My own sake and remember your sins no more" (Isa. 43:25). "I have swept away your transgressions like a cloud and your sins like a mist" (Isa. 44:22). Therefore, make us quick to return to You, for You have redeemed us. Make us as eager to wear Your righteousness and holiness as You are to wear our sins. I feel Lord, that I am at a lose for words. I know I need to confess and repent daily but I don't. I wait until that sin has bogged me down and I am in the depths of despair. It seems like I have to wait for you to convict my heart to the point that I am hopeless. Help me Lord to learn to confess my sins everyday.

DAY 14

Waist-Deep in Glory

BEFORE YOU BEGIN
Read Matthew 3:13–15

STOP AND CONSIDER
But John tried to stop Him, saying,
"I need to be baptized by You, and yet You come to me" (v. 14).

What keeps far too many believers from being as humbled and overwhelmed by the presence of God as John was? *Pride - because people don't like to feel humble - they think it's a sign of weakness*

What changes could you make in your daily activities and typical priorities in order to cultivate a heart that continues to be stunned by His willingness to stoop to our level?

I need to stop spending so much time on the computer and in front of the TV and spend time with God.

Our gloriously deliberate God orchestrated the lives of two extraordinary men, born six months apart, to converge waist-deep in the waters of the Jordan River. For John the Baptizer, it was the beginning of the end. He had prepared God's way, and now God was preparing his. For Jesus, it marked the end of the beginning. His life would descend on Galilee, Judea, and Jerusalem like a desert storm. That day in the river of promise, John baptized Jesus with water, and Jesus baptized the Jordan with glory.

Just imagine what was going on in the mind of Christ as He was walking to the river Jordan. I wonder if He stopped to watch the scene for awhile, with the people confessing their sins. Did He watch this mighty servant of God preaching the Word with boldness? I'm just picturing somehow that horizon and His figure overlooking the scene. Then He walks up to the shore, and John sees Him.

I've written something that is strictly fiction. I was just reflecting on what might have been going through John's mind as Jesus approached him. Perhaps these thoughts will help us see again what happens when very real people encounter the Son of God:

"My tongue had been like a flame that day. The Word of God came to me in the desert like fire from heaven. If I hadn't preached it, it would have consumed me. I had no fear. No intimidation. God sent me to those Jordan waters, and I knew they'd come. No prearranged meeting. Just the wind of the Spirit wooing, drawing, then blowing away the debris of sin, preparing the way for the Deliverer. No matter who came to the shore to hear or to jeer. The message was immutable, "Repent! For the kingdom of heaven is near!"

"The fruit of repentance pierced the wind with cries of confession and waves of grief. I hardly stepped out of those waters that day. My voice grew raspy and hoarse but never quiet. Boldness was the marrow in my bones. Funny how stunned we are when the future we prophesy suddenly becomes present. I had told them I was unworthy to loose His sandals and that I would only baptize with water for repentance. He would baptize with

the Holy Spirit and with fire. I spoke like an authority. Like an associate of the closest kind. Like someone who knew it all. I didn't.

"I was just raising a repentant man from the waters when I saw someone out of the corner of my eye walk to the water's edge. As I think back, how those waters kept from parting that day, I'll never know. Numbers were gathered on the shore. Others were waist-deep in the water. Suddenly I became oblivious to all but the overpowering presence of the One. There He stood, looking straight at me, through me. Oh, it was Him all right! I had been preparing for Him all my life, and yet I was not ready. All I could do was look at Him and shake my head, 'No. Please, no! Not me. I have need to be baptized by You!'

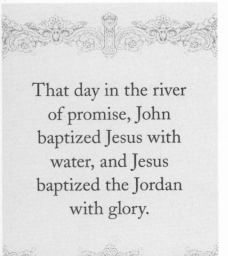

That day in the river of promise, John baptized Jesus with water, and Jesus baptized the Jordan with glory.

"Suddenly I was overcome by my own compulsion to flood the shore with waves of repentance, and He answered, 'Let it be for now. It is proper for us to do this to fulfill all righteousness.' So I consented, shaking all over. I placed my left hand on His back and my right hand on His chest. I felt the heartbeat of the Son of God. As if in slow motion, I leaned Him back into those waters, His weight submitting to my hands.

"All of a sudden the Jordan chilled me to the bone. I raised Him from the waters, and He stood before me drenched in the river of promise. The water dripping from His beard seemed to drop like diamonds, proclaiming His endless perfections. He alone had no confessions to make that day. Only one was made over Him, the confession of His holiness enthroned in heaven. 'This is my Son whom I love and with Him I am well pleased.' The blessing of the Father fell like a dove from heaven. He walked out of those waters and into our lives, interrupting a fallen world with grace and truth. My name is John. I am the son of a simple man and woman. I baptized the Messiah that day."

Can you imagine? He had prepared all his life. When we set apart our lives unto Him, He will do wonders with us the likes of which we cannot imagine.

I've left you plenty of room today so you could try to recapture what it was like when you first met the Christ. How did He seem to you? What was it like? How does He still amaze you at times with the sheer glory and wonder—and stark reality—of His presence?

It's been twenty-one years since I first met Jesus. I was seven years old, but I don't remember what it was like. Fifteen years later, I rededicated my life back to God and then I felt peace. There have been times since then that I have fallen from God, then gotten close. (This is a neverending cycle.) God still amazes me. It will just show Himself to me and I am captured by His presence. I am in all and the tears of joy and peace flow from me.

Praying God's Word Today

Lord Jesus, to see You today in glory—your head and hair white like wool, Your feet like fine bronze fired in a furnace, Your voice like the sound of cascading waters, Your face shining like the sun at midday—I, like John the apostle, fall on my face as though dead (Rev. 1:14–17). Your boundless beauty and majesty astound me. May it ever be so!

Lord Jesus, I want to feel Your
presence every day. I want to
feel the joy and peace that it brings.
I want to fall at Your feet and
praise You.
Lord, I need to feel Your presence
today. I need to know that You are
with me. I cannot handle this
class without You. Please pour Your
Spirit into the 5th grade today
Please show them You are the
reason we live and breath. Help
me to guide them to You. Help me
to train and discipline them in
the right way.

DAY 15

A Father Unlike His Son

Before You Begin
Read Matthew 3:16–17

Stop and Consider
The heavens suddenly opened up for Him, and He saw the Spirit of God
descending like a dove and coming down on Him (vv. 16–17).

Why isn't heaven always open to our sight? What is the benefit of knowing it's there—and
knowing He's there—without being able to physically see for ourselves? *Its Called*
Faith.

Whether you feel like you've received your father's blessing or not, describe the importance
of this in a person's life. What goes missing when it's not given? What comes pouring
through when it is? *My father is very important in*
my life because he helps guide me. He's
always there when something goes wrong.
He's also their just to love me.

Back in Genesis 1, God created the heavens and the earth, He separated the expanse from the waters, and He called that expanse the sky. I can't help but think, then, "If He called it into being and put it in its place, He can open it if He wants to!" On the day when Jesus was baptized, the Father opened up the sky like a window, and showed Christ the vision through it.

This event makes me think of Stephen, the very first martyr, because heaven was opened to him and he saw Jesus Christ standing at the right hand of God on his behalf. What I want you to understand is that heaven is right there. We look up at that sky at night and the expanse of the stars. He is literally just an open window away from us, sitting on His throne. His presence is in us and on us. God upon His throne is near. We just can't quite see it yet.

On this special occasion God did something unusual. He opened up that window, and Christ looked straight into heaven. It had been a long time since He had seen that vision. I believe part of God's purpose for sending Jesus here was to experience life as we do. That means I don't believe He had X-ray vision every single second into the throne room of God. I believe that many times He prayed, meditated, and had relationship with His Father in the very same ways we do today. So what a time this must have been to capture that moment when He could see heaven open and the Holy Spirit descend.

And then to hear His Father's blessing. Again, I don't think God spoke audibly to His Son every day He was on earth. I think maybe Jesus was called here to sympathize with us and to take part in the kind of relationship we do. A whole lot of His prayer was spent talking to God, knowing only in His own Spirit and through God's Word what the Father was answering Him. So the audible voice of His Father sounding forth at His baptism must have just fallen on Jesus with the dearest of familiarity. This was the love of His life. I want to think that through the night, He replayed that voice and blessing in His own mind a thousand times. "He loves Me. Life is hard here, but He's proud of Me. I have the blessing. I have the blessing."

PRAYING GOD'S WORD TODAY

Lord Jesus, lest I ever forget, You are the image of the invisible God, the firstborn over all creation; because by You, everything was created in heaven and on earth, the visible and the invisible, whether thrones or dominions or rulers or authorities—all things have been created through You and for You. You are before all things, and by You all things hold together (Col. 1:15–17). Dear Heavenly Father, You are the loving Father. You are Glorious and magnificent. You created all things for You. Help me to realize this as I step into to the classroom today and look at each Child. I need to realize that You made each one and that You put me in this room to help guide each Child. Please reveal Your presence to us so that we may follow You.

DAY 16

Tempting Invitations

BEFORE YOU BEGIN
Read Luke 4:1–13

STOP AND CONSIDER
Jesus returned from the Jordan, full of the Holy Spirit, and was led by the Spirit
in the wilderness for 40 days to be tempted by the Devil (vv. 1–2).

Why would God lead His Son into the desert immediately following His baptism? _____

So He could fast and pray and prepare
Himself for His ministry

What have been some of your most obvious "wilderness" seasons? Do you remember what
preceded them? How did they change you? _There have been_
several times that I have had
"wilderness" seasons. When I was looking
for answers from God on where to
Go next in life. Each one drew me closer
to God.

Christ's experience in the desert represented an intense season of temptation that was tailored by the enemy for the challenges of messiahship that lay ahead. God placed Jesus with His adversary in a lab of sorts to establish the ground rules from the very beginning. With this idea in mind, let's briefly consider each temptation:

1) *"Tell this stone to become bread" (v. 3)*. Could Christ turn a stone into bread? Undoubtedly! So why shouldn't He? After all, He was famished. Matthew 4:2 tells us He had been fasting for forty days. Nothing is wrong with eating when a person is hungry—unless a greater issue is involved. Most likely Jesus' intent in fasting was to seek God and refrain from all distractions, much the same way Anna, the prophetess, was said to serve God "night and day, fasting and praying" (Luke 2:37). Since we know Jesus was filled with the Spirit and led by the Spirit, we can assume the Spirit prompted the fast; therefore, the fast wasn't over until God said so.

What did this temptation have to do with Christ's imminent ministry? Robert Stein says the issue was whether or not Christ would use His power for His own ends. "Would He live by the same requirements of faith and dependence on God as everyone else in the kingdom?"[2] Satan's strategy wasn't all that different from what he used when tempting Eve in the garden (see Gen. 3:1). In both cases, Satan wanted to sow doubt, but not because he had any. He knew what God had said to Adam and Eve, and he definitely knew Christ was the Son of God. Why in the world would Satan have tried sowing doubt in Christ?

We see a second similarity between the Garden of Eden and the wilderness, in that both temptations involved food. Christ was hungry. Eve was hungry, too, even though her hunger was for something different. Our appetites are ferocious. They are fodder for much temptation. I find Paul's description of the enemies of the cross of Christ very interesting in Philippians 3:19 when he said their minds are on earthly things and "their god is their stomach." Although you and I are not enemies of the cross, we certainly know the temptation of making our stomachs gods. But Christ didn't fall to this temptation. Instead He responded with two critical phrases.

Christ's first phrase of response was universal, because Scripture applies to every temptation we can ever face. He said, "It is written" (Luke 4:4). In those words He clarified the matter of authority. Jesus subjugated Satan's words to God's Word.

The second phrase of Jesus' response was issue-specific. "Man must not live on bread alone." Christ applied the specific word from Scripture to meet His need. So Satan moved on to the next temptation.

2) *"If you worship me, it will all be yours" (v. 7)*. We cannot imagine Christ ever being the least bit tempted to worship Satan, but can we not imagine that He might have been tempted to rip Satan's authority out of his hands?

Christ didn't challenge Satan's ability to *make* such an offer. We can assume Satan must have had the authority as the prince of this world. It's true the authority God has allowed Satan is limited and temporary, but it is nonetheless very real.

> Before Christ went public, He had to determine what type of Messiah He was going to be. Some issues were meant to be settled from the beginning.

Yet can you imagine how Christ must feel as He watches the state of the world under the influence of the evil prince's authority? Oppression, violence, and deception characterize the world God loves. Surely Christ is counting the days until He grabs the deed restriction to the world and reigns without rival in righteousness.

Satan was hoping Christ would be so anxious to secure the world that He'd worship him. Needless to say, Satan was wrong. Christ will most assuredly reign over this world, but not until all things have happened according to God's kingdom calendar.

Once again Christ called on Scripture, this time with the specific application: "Worship the Lord your God, and serve him only" (v. 8). Christ adamantly resisted worshiping Satan as a way to gain the world. So Satan moved to his third temptation.

3) *"Throw yourself down from here"* (v. 9). Based on Christ's response to this temptation, we know that at least one of Satan's intentions was to tempt Christ to put God to the test. But Satan may have had a second intention in this particular temptation. The placement of the temptation at the temple suggests that the enemy may have been hoping a dramatic scene would cause the Jews to hail Jesus as their king before He faced the cross. If Christ had foregone the cross, He would have been no less God, but we would be lost.

In conclusion, it's clear that these were no ordinary temptations. They appear to be direct assaults on the messiahship of Christ. We can, however, draw a few applications from them:

• Seasons of intense temptation are not indications of God's displeasure.

• Satan is tenacious. Don't expect him to give up after one or two tries.

• Scripture is the most powerful tool in our fight against temptation. Don't fight back with *your* words. Fight back with God's!

What are some of the patterns you've observed in the way temptations come to you? How can that help you be better prepared to deal with them? When I am sitting at home and doing nothing, temptation creeps up. Also when I am frustrated, Satan will tempt me to "loose my head." I can deal with these when I spend time w/ God every day.

Praying God's Word Today

Lord, I am so grateful that we do not have a high priest who is unable to sympathize with our weaknesses, but One who has been tested in every way as we are, yet without sin (Heb. 4:15). Therefore, I cling to the promise that no temptation has overtaken us except what is common to humanity. You are faithful, Lord, and will not allow us to be tempted beyond what we are able to bear. In fact, with the temptation You will also provide a way of escape, so that we may be able to bear it (1 Cor. 10:13). *Lord Jesus, each day I am tempted in someway. Whether it be food, the mind, or emmotions. Help me Lord to overcome this temptations. I need Your strength and quidance. Help me to remember Your word during these times.*

DAY 17

Proclaiming Provision

BEFORE YOU BEGIN
Read Luke 4:14–21

STOP AND CONSIDER

He began by saying to them, "Today as you listen, this Scripture has been fulfilled" (v. 21).

What have you been living with (or living without)—not fully comprehending all that Christ has come to be and to do in you? _____

_____

_____

We all face inevitable suffering and difficulty in life. How can we square this with the reality that Christ has called us to thrive, not merely survive? *Christ has called us to thrive in our Christian life. The suffering and difficulty in our lives, leads us closer to Him.*

_____

I was a mess before the Savior set me free. That's why my dearest life passages are the ones found in Isaiah 61:1–2 and quoted again in the Gospel of Luke. Jesus went to His home synagogue in Nazareth and declared both the fact and the nature of His call and ministry—to preach good news to the poor . . . to heal the brokenhearted . . . to proclaim freedom for the prisoners . . . sight for the blind . . . to release the oppressed . . . and to proclaim the year of the Lord's favor (Luke 4:18–19). Let's briefly discuss each part of that description:

1) *"The Spirit of the Lord is on me, because he has anointed me to preach good news to the poor" (Luke 4:18).* Christ didn't mean the financially destitute. The Greek word for "poor" is *ptochos,* indicating "utter helplessness, complete destitution, afflicted, distressed." I think God is far too faithful to let anyone make it through life without confronting seasons of utter helplessness. Sooner or later, any healthy individual discovers that autonomy doesn't cut it. Like beggars we go from person to person with our empty cup, crying, "Can't you add anything to my life?" They might throw in a coin or two. But when we shake the cup, the tinny echo reminds us how empty we remain. Until we allow Jesus to fill our cups daily, we simply subsist. Sooner or later, God will make sure we confront the poverty of living on the alms of others so that we may learn to feast on Him.

2) *"To heal the brokenhearted" (Luke 4:18 KJV).* Some New Testament translations include this phrase, while others don't. Either way, it is worthy of our consideration. The original word for "brokenhearted" is *suntribo,* meaning "to break, strike against something . . . to break the strength or power of someone." The Greek word for "heal" is *iaomai,* meaning "to heal, cure, restore." I love the Hebrew word translated "heal" in Exodus 15:26 when God introduced Himself by a new title: "I am the LORD who heals you." The word *raphah* means "to mend (by stitching), repair thoroughly, make whole." I picture God focusing steadily on the object of repair. One stitch follows another. It takes time. I picture painful penetrations of the healing needle. I don't know about you, but I'm quite sure if my healing processes had been painless, I would have relapsed.

3) "To proclaim freedom for the prisoners" (v. 18). Long after my salvation, I was in many ways like the prisoners in Psalm 107:10–16, 20, suffering "in iron chains, for they had rebelled against the words of God" (vv. 10–11). Many people sincerely love God, but I don't think anyone stands to appreciate the unfailing love of God like the believer finally set free from failure. I know this captive can undoubtedly testify: He sent forth His Word and healed me. Stitch by stitch. But please notice that Christ *proclaimed* freedom. He didn't impose it. It remains an offer.

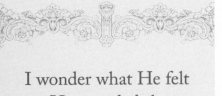

I wonder what He felt as He rounded those familiar hills and gazed upon his hometown village, no longer as a fellow citizen but as a saving servant.

4) "Recovery of sight for the blind" (v. 18). Although Christ would heal many from physical blindness, I believe His intent here was a far more serious kind of blindness. Second Corinthians 4:4 says, "The god of this age has blinded the minds of unbelievers, so they cannot see the light of the gospel of the glory of Christ, who is the image of God."

I find the original word for "blind" in both Luke's Gospel and Paul's second letter to the Corinthians to be so interesting. *Tuphlos* means "to envelop with smoke, to be unable to see clearly." Perhaps none of the enemy's attempts to cloud our vision compare to our fiery trials. His job is to keep us blinded to the One who walks with us through the fire. Oh, believer, God is there whether our spiritual eyes discern Him or not.

5) "To release the oppressed" (v. 18). I looked up every definition for "oppressed" in the Greek and Hebrew dictionaries. A half dozen original words are translated in the Bible with our single word "oppressed," and all but one have the word "break" in the definition. I'm becoming more and more convinced that heavy-duty oppression is Satan's counterfeit for biblical brokenness.

At times I've fought back the tears as I've heard testimonies of people who had been utterly unable to function, describing themselves as broken by God. I don't think God's

brand of brokenness is total emotional wreckage. God's intent in breaking us is to bend our stiff knees so that we will submit to His authority and take on His yoke. His aim is our abundant and effective life. Being totally unable to function because the mind and emotions are in shambles is Satan's counterfeit. Praise God, Christ can certainly use Satan's counterfeit brokenness to bring us to a place of accepting His own, but I think we credit some things to Christ that He doesn't do.

6) *"To proclaim the year of the Lord's favor" (v. 19)*. Those who gathered that year in the Nazarene synagogue were staring in the face of the Lord's favor—His blessed gift of grace, Jesus Christ. The word "year" can be translated as "any definite time." God places before each of us a definitive period of time to accept the Lord's favor. He wills for none to perish but for all to come to repentance (see 2 Pet. 3:9). The world has until His return. The individual has a definitive period of time known by God alone. I am not past begging people not to wait too long for salvation, because eternal life in heaven is at stake. Neither am I beyond begging them to embrace His freedom, because abundant life on earth is at stake. He longs to be your champion now.

What do you find most precious and personal in these descriptions of Jesus? *I find that Jesus is there with us no matter what happens in our lives.*

PRAYING GOD'S WORD TODAY

Lord, You have said to the prisoners, "Come out!" And to those who are in darkness, "Be free!" Therefore, because of Your grace and power, we will feed along the pathways and will find pasture even on the barren heights. We will no longer hunger or thirst, and the scorching heat of the sun will not strike us, for our compassionate One will guide us and will lead us to springs of water (Isa. 49:9–10). *Lord Jesus, you have put me into some difficult situations and sometimes I have failed and other times I have glorified you. As I am going through these events in my life now, help me to follow as you. Guide me to the directions you want me to go. I want to do your will Lord.*

DAY 18

Shooting Stars

BEFORE YOU BEGIN
Read Luke 4:22–30

STOP AND CONSIDER

They were all speaking well of Him and were amazed by the gracious words
that came from His mouth, yet they said, "Isn't this Joseph's son?" (v. 22).

Why do people in the religious world make idols, stars, and celebrities out of Christian
singers and speakers? *Because we expect them to be a "perfect Christian," so we put them on a pedistal.*

In what regular situations do you face the adult version of "peer pressure," having to make
the choice between being yourself and being who others want you to be? *In work situation, people expect you to be a certain way. Also in church.*

The translation "spoke well of" in Luke 4:22 comes from the Greek word *martureo*, meaning "to be a witness, bear witness . . . to be able or ready to testify." "Amazed" is the Greek word *thaumazo*, meaning "struck with admiration." Either of these words could be used by spectators after attending any rock concert and being impressed by a talent. The wording suggests that they were impressed by Christ's delivery—not so much what He said, but how He said it.

Let me draw on my experience and offer a possible explanation. After delivering a message, nothing hits me like cold water more than someone saying, "You are a great speaker." First of all, I know better than that. I have a thick accent and use tons of country colloquialisms. Far more importantly, though, if someone makes a statement like that, I know either I failed miserably or the person didn't get it. In the case of Jesus' teaching, we know He can't fail, so obviously, they didn't get it. In Jesus' seemingly harsh words (vv. 24–27), He may have been responding to their grading His speech rather than receiving His message.

Notice also a second consideration: the velocity of the crowd's change of mood. The crowd's mood went from admiration to a murderous rage in the moments of Christ's confrontation. Luke describes them as furious (v. 28). The word in the text for "furious" comes from the word *thuo*, meaning "to move impetuously, particularly as the air or wind, a violent motion or passion of the mind." The north wind of their admiration suddenly reversed into a south wind of tornadic proportions. When a mood can change in a matter of moments from admiration to murderous fury, something is amiss.

The types of crowds Christ encountered two thousand years ago still fill many churches today. Many congregations want to hear impressive A+ messages, but the messenger better keep his confrontational thoughts to himself. The same committee that throws out the red carpet to a new preacher may eventually roll him out the door in it! Meanness at church sometimes exceeds anything that occurs in secular surroundings. As James 3:10 says, "My brethren, these things ought not so to be" (KJV).

PRAYING GOD'S WORD TODAY

Lord Jesus, as we see You driven by the angry mobs to the edge of town, threatened with death by those who once gave you flattery and praise, we are reminded that You suffered outside the gate so that You might sanctify us by Your blood. Therefore, we come to You outside the gate, bearing Your disgrace. For here we do not have an enduring city; instead, we seek the one to come (Heb. 13:12–14). Lord, Help me to not to make idols our of Christian singers. You put them in those positions to minister to others. Help me to focus on the meaning of the message and not the rhythme or beat. Also Lord, help me to focus on Your words.

DAY 19

The Enemy's
True Colors

JESUS

BEFORE YOU BEGIN
Read Luke 4:31–37

STOP AND CONSIDER
In the synagogue there was a man with an unclean
demonic spirit who cried out with a loud voice, "Leave us alone!
What do You have to do with us, Jesus—Nazarene" (vv. 33–34).

Have you ever observed clear demonic activity? What were its most noticeable indications and characteristics? _____

_____

_____

What are some things you know about Satan from the Scripture? (If nothing comes to mind, read Ezekiel 28:11–17, Isaiah 14:12–15, and Revelation 12:3–12.) _Satan_

was is very prideful, was thrown out of Heaven

_____

_____

Christ's earthly ministry had hardly been launched before the demonic world confronted Him—in a synagogue, no less. Thank goodness, Christ isn't spooked by the demonic world. No matter what authority Satan and his subjects have been temporarily allowed in this world system, Christ can pull rank any time He wants. On that day in Capernaum, He wasted no time. A demon-possessed man shouted loudly and declared Jesus to be the Holy One of God.

The demon appeared to desire attention. We can assume the demon was loud because Christ adamantly told him to "Be quiet!" I'm certainly not suggesting that all demonic activity is loud. I am asking you to consider that when allowed to penetrate a place meant for practices of devotion to God, one of the chief tactics of demons is to divert attention.

I've seen this tactic. At a recent conference a woman began to shriek right after someone prayed and before I was to speak. The wise and godly woman leading the conference immediately went to the microphone and dealt graciously but firmly with the outburst. Although I've not often observed that type of behavior, the few times I've experienced it, I discerned a tactic of the demonic world to divert attention.

Note that the demon seemed to be telling some semblance of the truth, but we see a distortion or misuse of the truth in the demonic testimony. He was acting as a counterfeit preacher of sorts. He could not stop the truth so he hoped to disqualify the message by the instability or insanity of the apparent messenger.

Some years ago, a strange thing happened at our church. Each Sunday, for six or seven weeks, a man who appeared to be mentally ill would stand outside the main doors and "preach" to us using a megaphone as we left the building after worship. Some of the statements he made were technically scriptural, but his appearance and his approach demonstrated such instability that he did more to distract people from the truth than attract. The typical listener's tendency would be to disbelieve anything he said simply because he was the one saying it.

Noise and distraction. These remain some of the enemy's stock-in-trade.

Praying God's Word Today

Father, I am thankful to You for exposing Satan as the liar and deceiver he truly is. I know we must expect his noise and distraction for now as he desperately (and unsuccessfully) tries to avoid his fate. But I hear another noise—the sound of uproar from the city! A voice from the temple—the voice of the Lord, paying back Your enemies what they deserve (Isa. 66:6). Oh, how I long to see that day! Lord, help me to fight against Satan. I'm struggling with it and so are my students. Help me to find a way that we can overpower Him. Help us to remember to put on the armor of God and help us to remember that You are in control and that we need to keep our eyes on You.

DAY 20

House Calls

BEFORE YOU BEGIN
Read Mark 1:29–34

STOP AND CONSIDER

As soon as they left the synagogue, they went into Simon and
Andrew's house with James and John. Simon's mother-in-law was lying
in bed with a fever, and they told Him about her at once (vv. 29–30).

How present is Jesus in the everyday routine of your household? How much of your relationship with Him takes place within your home and within the interaction of your family?

*Since I live by myself, I need to let
Jesus be more of a routine in my house*

What would it be like if meeting with Jesus always required going to another place, leaving
our homes to go out looking for Him? *I can look at this
two ways 1) the most common, I'd
just stay @ home 2) If I had to leave the
house, it might encourage me to go booty.*

What a relief to know that God doesn't just go to church, He goes to our homes! When I was a little girl, I was fairly certain God lived in our church baptistry. My vivid imagination turned dressing-room doors into secret passages that led into the mysterious dwelling of the divine boogie man. I am happy to report, though, that God doesn't live in the baptistry. He lives in the hearts of those who trust Him and in the homes of those who provide Him room.

Sometimes, though, we don't bother to summon Jesus Christ into our homes until we are overwhelmed by threatening circumstances.

Do you have a sense of Christ's activity in your home? I've a good reason for asking you this question. Almost every spiritual marker of Christ's heightened activity in my home came as a direct result of some threatening situation. Right now both my daughters are walking with God, but I assure you this did not simply happen in the natural evolution of their lives. I watched their relationships grow over the years they shared our home, through situations in which some threat convinced them to cleave closer to Christ.

When Jesus went to help Simon's mother-in-law, Luke 4:39 tells us He "bent over her." I don't think I'm reading too much into the picture to imagine a close encounter suggesting deep concern. I always reacted in a similar way any time one of my children was sick. I didn't remain upright and stoic, checking off a list of symptoms. I bent over them and drew close. I had learned from my mother that I could better gauge a temperature with my cheek on their foreheads than with a thermometer. I could not keep my distance from a sick child, even if her malady was contagious.

Christ could have healed Simon's mother-in-law from the front porch. He didn't. He came to her and drew down close. After all, she was in no position to seek help for herself. He involved Himself one-on-one with those He helped.

Our homes today are threatened by fevers of all sorts—far beyond the physiological: unresolved conflict, unforgiveness, unfaithfulness, compromising media communications, pornography, and more. We need Jesus in our homes.

PRAYING GOD'S WORD TODAY

Who is like You, Lord God—the One enthroned on high, who stoops down to look on the heavens and the earth? You raise the poor from the dust, and You lift the needy from the garbage pile in order to seat us with nobles (Ps. 113:5–8). You have come into our lives and into our homes. Make Yourself welcome, I pray. Lord, I need to make You more of an important feature in my home. I need to go to You even when I'm not facing difficult circumstances. Help Me to get My priorities Right, And have You more in My home.

DAY 21

Jesus in the Morning,
Jesus in the Evening

BEFORE YOU BEGIN

Read Mark 1:35–39

STOP AND CONSIDER

*Very early in the morning, while it was still dark, He got up, went out,
and made His way to a deserted place. And He was praying there (v. 35).*

Is there a certain time of day when you find your time with the Lord particularly sweet and tangible? Describe what makes it that way. *It's in the evening right before bed. This way I can think on Him and cast away my worries*

What thoughts or activities interrupt your ability to escape the way Jesus did, intent on spending time with the Father, desiring Him more than anything else? *TV, Computer, worries - all these things interrupt my ability to spend time w/ Jesus.*

Two times of day; two fascinating looks at our Jesus—the One and Only.

Luke 4:40 tells us that the sick and suffering came out to see Jesus "when the sun was setting." To those of us who are Gentiles, the reason for this is not so obvious. Christ had previously left the synagogue when He went to the home of Simon, meaning it was the Sabbath day. Remember, at this point Christ primarily had been ministering in various synagogues to Jews. It was unlawful for them to carry the sick on the Sabbath. But God-fearing people counted the moments until the sun set over the Sea of Galilee, marking the close of day. So as the darkness fell, they bundled their sick and brought them to the Light. The thought almost makes me cry. It was as if they watched the clock of the law tick until it finally struck grace . . . and they raced to Him with their need. How blessed we are to live in the liberty of a completed Calvary! The pharmacy dispensing God's grace is open 24/7.

But a second snapshot of time also appears in our passage. Early the next morning, Jesus rose and went out to pray (Mark 1:35). I wish I had words to express the feelings such scriptural moments stir in me. The thought of Christ ducking out the door while it was still dark to find a place to be by Himself with God floods my soul with emotion. I love every glimpse of the unique relationship Father and Son shared while Christ was on earth and His Father was in heaven. Never before had such a bridge connected the celestial and the terrestrial. I always wonder what Christ said to His Father and what He heard in those intimate moments. Did God the Father speak audibly to Him? Or did He speak in His heart like He does to you and me through His Word? I can't wait to find out someday in glory.

We have no idea how often Jesus got to steal away with His Father, but Scripture says He was soon interrupted by his disciples, excitedly shouting, "Everyone is looking for you!" (v. 37). I'm convinced we don't give enough thought to how challenging Jesus' prison of flesh must have felt to Him. Prior to His advent, He was completely unencumbered by the natural laws governing the human body. Suddenly He experienced for Himself the pull to be in many places at once and the challenge to prioritize not just the good but the goal: proclaiming the good news of the kingdom of God. "That is why I have come" (v. 38).

PRAYING GOD'S WORD TODAY

Father, we know that Your hand is gracious to all who seek You, but that Your anger burns against all who abandon You (Ezra 8:22). May we, like Your people throughout history—and like Jesus when He walked on the earth—seek You while You may be found and call to You while You are near. Let us abandon our wicked, sinful thoughts, and let us return to You, Lord, so that we may know Your heart and receive Your compassion (Isa. 55:6–7).

Lord, I need to seek You more,
I need to get rid of the
interruptions and focus on
You. Give me the strength &
ability to fight against the
flesh and the idols I put
before You.

DAY 22

*Fighting for
First Place*

Before You Begin
Read Matthew 4:23–25

Stop and Consider

Jesus was going all over Galilee, teaching in their synagogues, preaching the good news of the kingdom, and healing every disease and sickness among the people (v. 23).

What worthy activities or pursuits often lure you away from your main priorities? _____

TV and Computer

What answer could you give to those who think you're being lazy or indifferent by not sharing the same zeal they possess for some cause or ministry or emphasis? _____

God calls people to do different things and this cause I may not be lead to have a passion for.

Luke's recap of this same event in chapter 4 concludes with a definitive statement: "He kept on preaching in the synagogues of Judea" (v. 44). *He kept on*—no matter how many directions He felt pulled. No matter how many needs remained in each town. No matter what others prioritized for Him—"He kept on." Why? Because every other need humanity possessed was secondary to the need to hear and receive the gospel. Not unimportant, mind you. Just secondary. Physical healing affects this life alone, but the kingdom is forever.

Then why did Christ spend time and energy performing miracles of healing on such temporal bodies? Probably for three primary reasons:

1) Because He could. He can do whatever He wants. Before that fact makes you nervous, remember: what He wants is always consistent with who He is. Among many other wonderful things, He is the healer. In one way or another, He heals every single person who comes to Him by faith.

2) Because He is compassionate—beyond anything we can imagine.

3) Because the miracles helped authenticate the messenger.

Preaching the good news of the kingdom of God was Christ's absolute priority. One of the biggest temptations even mature believers face is being sidetracked by the urgent. Many situations need our attention. They tempt us to let them steal our focus. Christ may have faced the same temptation when the people came to Him and tried to "keep him from leaving them" (Luke 4:42). The people's attempts to hold onto Christ may not have been limited to just the vocal and emotional. They may have hung onto Him physically too. How His heart must have broken for them. Yet He knew the best thing He could do for them was to stay true to His mission.

Can you imagine how Jesus longed for the time when His work would be accomplished and He could dwell within the hearts of all who would receive Him, never to leave them? Until then, He had a job to do. Christ ignored neither the urgent need nor the ultimate goal—but He never allowed the former to hinder the latter.

PRAYING GOD'S WORD TODAY

Lord, please help us pay careful attention to our life's walk—not as unwise people but as wise—making the most of the time. I realize that the days are evil and filled with temptations, which not only entice us to sin but also to mistake activity for purpose. So help us not to be foolish but to understand what Your will is (Eph. 5:15–17).

Lord, Help me to pay attention to the way you want me to live and do my job. Help me to keep my eyes focused on you and not the things of the world.

DAY 23

Lessons from
a Fish Tale

Before You Begin

Read Luke 5:1–11

Stop and Consider

He and all those with him were amazed at the catch of fish they took, and
so were James and John, Zebedee's sons, who were Simon's partners (vv. 9–10).

When was the last time you were "amazed" at something Jesus did through you, knowing
there was no other explanation for it? _____

_____

_____

Think about the subtle differences between working "for" Jesus and working "with" Him.
What does working "with" Jesus look like in real life? *If I am working
"with" Jesus, then I am happy and
willing to do what He ask because we
are working together.*

THE ONE AND ONLY

Today we celebrate a fact that continually staggers my imagination: Christ calls mere mortals to join Him in His work. Trust me, He doesn't *need* our help. Christ could save the world through dreams and visions if He chose to. But He doesn't. He delights in asking us to join Him. I am convinced that every believer is summoned by Christ to work with Him here on earth. In fact, we learn a lot about how and why He does it by observing this encounter between Jesus and Peter on the lake in Luke 5:

1) Christ knows more about our jobs than we do. Jesus told Peter how to fish. Now, had Peter not already known Christ, he might have thought: "Me fisherman, You carpenter. I won't tell You how to build, and You don't tell me how to fish." Instead, he submitted with only one brief disclaimer: "We've done this all night and caught nothing."

One of the most critical reasons believers experience defeat is because we categorize only a few areas of our lives as Christ's arena. Many Christians think Christ's jurisdiction doesn't extend into certain areas. So, as if to save Him the extra trouble of dealing with things that don't concern Him, they leave Christ at church to deal with areas related to His expertise.

Satan is greatly defeated when we start living the truth that every area is Christ's specialty. Whether you're a homemaker, steelworker, or CEO, Christ knows every detail associated with your job. Jesus knows accounting, movie-theater managing, banking, drafting, engineering, nursing, real-estate brokering, and anything else we could do. For crying out loud, the One who knows the numbers of hairs on your head could also style them if He wanted. Not one of us does anything for a living that He can't do better.

2) Christ honors our submission even when our only motivation is obedience. If there was one phrase I wasn't going to say as a parent, it was "Because I said so." I heard those words from my Army captain dad more times than I could count. I wasn't about to repeat them. After all, I had studied child development. I vowed to explain things to my children as if they were little adults. I almost got away with it too. Then I had Melissa—the proverbial "But, why?" child. One day she pushed me too far, and something in me snapped. I suddenly exploded, "Because I said so!" Not just once. I screamed it over and over like a mad bull on a rampage. I even screamed it at the dog. Four-year-old Melissa shrugged her shoulders, said "OK!" and skipped off happily.

I called my dad and thanked him. Sometimes God allows us to explore the "whys" of His instructions. Other times He wants us to obey "because He said so." Then wait on the Lord to bless your act of obedience, no matter how long it takes. He is faithful.

> I don't just commit sin. Apart from God, I am sinful. My problem is not just what I do; it's who I am without His nature.

3) *The same job subjected to Christ's authority can yield entirely different results.* Peter surely had fished in every level of water in the lake. The key to his enormous catch was not the deep water Jesus had instructed him to fish in. It was simply the authority of Christ. Beloved, if your job has grown stale, you may not need a new occupation. You may just need a new partner. "Whatever you do, work at it with all your heart, as working for the Lord, not for men, since you know that you will receive an inheritance from the Lord as a reward. It is the Lord Christ you are serving" (Col. 3:23–24).

Every hour you do your job as working for the Lord gets punched on a time clock in heaven. You get paid by God Himself for the hours you work as unto the Lord. I'm not being cheesy. Our future inheritance is real, and it far exceeds minimum wage. As you partner with Christ at your job, you will be more efficient. No matter whether your new efficiency increases your earthly dividends or not, it most definitely will increase your *eternal* dividends, where moth and rust cannot destroy or thieves break in and steal (see Matt. 6:19).

4) *Christ's willingness to empower us can overwhelm us.* Simon Peter already knew Jesus possessed extraordinary power, but he felt the real impact of Christ's power when that

authority worked through his own hands. Suddenly the fisherman fell at Jesus' knees and said, "Go away from me, Lord; I am a sinful man" (Luke 5:8).

What blessed condescension that the God of glory would use us! And what humility this realization should bring! Peter was not prepared to receive his call until he had been confronted by his sin.

I have assuredly faced moments of such stark realization of my own sin that I felt unbearable pain. Interestingly, those moments did not come during times of rebellion, but rather, they came during close encounters with God when I drew close enough to get an eyeful of myself. Those realizations were both harrowing and liberating. The surrender resulting from the realization of my own innate unholiness did more to activate the holiness of God in me than anything I've ever experienced. How like God! Even our painful realizations of sinfulness are to mortify us to new life.

Recall an encounter you've had with Jesus that shed a harrowing and liberating light on you and your sinfulness. What brought this event about? How did it change you and your perspective on your relationship with Him? I don't have just one encounter, its actually several in one. The way I handle my classroom has shown me some sinfulness. Its the way I respond. As I have gotten closer to God, He has been trying to show me to act kinder and be His example.

PRAYING GOD'S WORD TODAY

O Father, You have told us in Your Word that if we search for You, we will find You—if we search for You with all of our heart and soul (Deut. 4:29). So today, we ask to be used in Your service, knowing that everyone who asks receives, and the one who searches finds, and to the one who knocks, the door to Your presence will be opened (Matt. 7:7–8).

Lord, I want to work with You in my job and everything in my life. Help me Lord to realize the things that I have done wrong and do the right thing. Help me to be a better teacher. For some reason, You have put me back in the classroom. Help me to be the best I can be because I know that You are my partner and that we will work together.

DAY 24

Healing for All
the Right Reasons

BEFORE YOU BEGIN
Read Luke 5:12–16

STOP AND CONSIDER

A man was there who had a serious skin disease all over him. He saw Jesus, fell facedown, and begged Him: "Lord, if You are willing, You can make me clean" (v. 12).

When you need a miracle, are you afraid to ask, not sure if it's God's will? Or do you feel confident asking Him to minister healing, trusting He will act according to His own plan and timing? How do you square these conflicts and questions in your mind and heart?

Sometimes I don't have enough faith. I always pray according to God will, but I need to have more faith and has for healing.

In what areas do you (or someone close to you) need His supernatural touch right now?

Me - Mental & Work

Hans - Cancer

This miracle from Luke 5 reveals a great deal of insight into God and His complex ways, helping us grapple with some challenging issues that question the hearts of men—questions we shouldn't be afraid of exploring as good students of the Word.

In essence, the leper was saying, "Lord, I know You possess the power to heal me. And if You in Your wisdom and plan see purpose in it, then please do it." So first, we see that the diseased man humbly approached Christ in absolute belief. Although he suffered from a horribly debilitating skin ailment, he did not suffer from a lack of faith. He believed Jesus could heal him. He just didn't know if he would.

This brings us, then, to a second consideration: was it in God's will to perform this miracle that the leper was asking for?

I believe with all my heart that the central issue involved in whether or not God heals a believing (see Matt. 9:28) and requesting (see James 4:2) Christian's physical illness is found in His eternal purpose. Although I don't pretend to understand how or why, some illnesses may serve more eternal purpose than healing would, while other healings serve more purpose than illnesses do.

Try as I might, I cannot imagine what purpose some illnesses and premature deaths serve. But after years of loving and seeking my God, I trust who He is, even when I have no idea what He's doing. Above all things, I believe God always has purpose in every decision He makes. Jesus healed people many times, but His healings were always with purpose and intent.

How much like the leper are you? Are you convinced (first of all) that Christ can do absolutely anything? And secondly, are you also seeking His purposes in everything? Are you more desirous of His work and will being done through your life than you are to be healed of your hardship or handicap? If so, don't lose courage. As long as this remains the desire of your heart, come to Christ as the leper did—humbly making your request while seeking His purposes for your life.

Praying God's Word Today

Lord God, as deeply as I desire Your health and healing—and believe in Your ability to provide it—I desire even more an abundance of Your peace and truth (Jer. 33:6). So hear my voice when I call. Be gracious to me and answer me. In Your behalf my heart says, "Seek My face." Your face, Lord, I will seek (Ps. 27:7–8). Lord, I believe in Your healing. I believe You can do miracles beyond miracles. Lord help me to have more faith because I know Your will, will be done.

DAY 25

Forgiveness Accepted

Before You Begin
Read Luke 5:17–26

Stop and Consider

"But so you may know that the Son of Man has authority on earth to forgive sins"—He told the paralyzed man—"I tell you: get up, pick up your stretcher, and go home" (v. 24).

What have you found to be the worst side-effects of sin, and what does Christ's forgiveness insert in their place? *The worst side affects of sins one is guilt. But God puts hope & peace in its place.*

Do you have a hard time accepting forgiveness—either God's or anyone else's? What do you believe is the source of your difficulty? *I have a hard time accepting God's forgivness because I feel guilty because I always end up doing it again because I have not kept my Faith & Trust in Jesus like I should.*

Jesus came as the Son of Man to rescue us from the great plight of man: we have a sin problem, and we are powerless to help ourselves. Given the right set of circumstances and the wrong state of mind, each of us is capable of just about anything. Even if we could get our external lives under perfect and legalistic control, we'd probably rot on the inside with the heinous sin of pride. Let's face it, we're all hopeless—except that Jesus came as the "Son of Man" with the "authority on earth to forgive sins."

I can remember being so devastated over a sin I had allowed to ensnare me that I repeatedly begged God to forgive me. I confessed my sin with great sorrow and turned radically from it. Still I continued to plead for forgiveness. Then one day in my Bible reading, God revealed these Scriptures to me from Luke 5. He spoke to my heart and said: "Beth, My child, you have an authority problem. You think you can do your part, which is repent. You just don't think I can do My part, which is forgive."

I was stunned. I began to realize that my sin of unbelief was as serious as my prior sin of rebellion. I wept and repented for my failure to credit Him with the authority He possessed to forgive my sins. It was eye-opening!

In his book *I Should Forgive, But . . .*, Dr. Chuck Lynch says when we keep confessing the same sin over and over, "each subsequent time the sin is confessed, rather than the confession bringing relief, it only reinforces the false belief that it has not been forgiven. Double, or re-confession, only deepens the false belief that we have not been forgiven."[3] I know he's right, because my constant re-confessions did not bring me relief. They only made me more miserable and self-loathing. Relief came only when I decided to take God at His Word.

If you have truly repented—which means you have experienced godly sorrow and a subsequent detour from the sin—bathe yourself in the river of God's forgiveness. The Son of Man has authority to forgive sins right here on earth. You don't have to wait until heaven. You can experience the freedom of complete forgiveness right here. Right now. Fall under Christ's authority and accept His grace.

Praying God's Word Today

Lord God, I behold Your face today with a shout of joy, knowing that You have restored Your righteousness in me. I can now tell others, "I have sinned and perverted what is right, yet I did not get what I deserved. For the Lord redeemed my soul from going down to the Pit, and I continue to see His light" (Job 33:26–28). Lord, I know I have doubted You and I ask for forgiveness. Help me to trust more in You. ~~xxxx~~ Help me work on my problems w/ Authority to You God. I know You will forgive me, just help me realize You do it immediately

DAY 26

Sitting By and
Finding Fault

BEFORE YOU BEGIN
Read Luke 6:1–11

STOP AND CONSIDER

The scribes and Pharisees were watching Him closely, to see if He would heal on the Sabbath, so that they could find a charge against Him (v. 7).

What are the fruits of a critical spirit, and why does it come so much easier to us than openness and a desire to seek understanding? *Proud, selfishness, boastful. It's easier to criticize someone because we look for fault to make ourselves look better*

True, we are commanded to be discerning. But what do we risk by being overly cautious and careful in our acceptance of Christian teaching? How do we draw the lines here?

I think we risk a personal relationship w/ Christ. We want to go over and beyond that we don't think of the person.

Back in Luke 5:17, the Pharisees and doctors of the law were seen "sitting by" while Jesus was teaching (KJV). Matthew Henry wrote, "How many are there in the midst of our assemblies, where the gospel is preached, that do not sit *under* the Word, but sit *by!* It is to them as a tale that is told them, not as a message that is sent them; they are willing that we should preach *before* them, but not that we should preach *to* them."[4]

Can you recall a time when you attended a Bible study or church service that profoundly affected a few of the people you were with, while others in attendance were completely unmoved? Like the Pharisees and teachers of the law, sometimes the unaffected can be the most "religious" people in the room. Could the difference be that they were sitting *by* rather than sitting *under* God's Word?

One of the stories in today's passage is proof positive of this.

On the Sabbath day, Jesus encountered a man with a withered right hand. Think of all the jobs that would have been difficult if not impossible for this man. A shepherd had to be adept at using a rod and a staff. A farmer needed both hands to plow. A carpenter had to hold a hammer in one hand and a nail in the other. A merchant would have had a difficult time securing and displaying goods with only one hand. Even a tax collector needed his right hand! So in the context of this event from Jesus' life, in which He would give a discourse on the issue of rest versus work, I don't think it was a coincidence that the man involved had lived a humiliating life of unwelcome "rest" from effective labor. Christ granted him rest on this day from his incapacity and futility. The One who created the Sabbath used it to bring restoration to a man weary of uselessness.

Meanwhile, however, the Pharisees and teachers of the law were "sitting by," watching Jesus, just looking for some basis to condemn Him. Their primary reason for attending was to see if Jesus would heal.

(By the way, I love the fact that they were convinced Christ would heal if He encountered someone in need—even on the Sabbath. What a healer He is! No amount of laws

could keep Him from being Himself! The Pharisees and teachers of the law caught Christ in the act of being God. Hallelujah!)

But by coming with the expressed intent of finding fault with Jesus, they proved that the most merciful people are those who have been sitting under the faucet of God's mercy instead of sitting by with a critical eye. Please note this sad fact, which was emphasized by the events following the Pharisees' and teachers' speculations: those who look for reasons to accuse will undoubtedly find some. They quickly found basis to accuse Jesus.

> If you will actively engage yourself in every message you hear or read, you will never hear or read another ineffective message.

In my own life and ministry, I've accepted the fact that anyone looking hard enough to condemn will sooner or later be accommodated. I really do believe that more people in the body of Christ are generally accepting than accusing, but one mean-spirited person is practically enough to ruin anyone's day. Francis Frangipane wrote something so powerful on this subject, I immediately committed it to memory. He said of the Lord:

> *To inoculate me from the praise of man,*
> *He baptized me in the criticism of man,*
> *until I died to the control of man.[5]*

Beloved, one thing I know for sure on this subject: nothing will squelch our efforts to seek the approval of others like not receiving it! Furthermore, those who approve of us one day can be the same ones who accuse us the next. I encourage you to break free from the traps set by approval and accusation. We are called to live our lives above reproach but to expect reproach anyway. Christ was blameless yet was blamed continually. I think you can trust me on this one: blameless people are rarely those who cast blame.

When the man with the shriveled hand stood before Him on the Sabbath, Jesus knew the Pharisees and teachers of the law were looking to accuse Him. But He did not allow Himself to be controlled by potential accusations nor even by the law that He Himself instituted. He was indeed the Lord of the Sabbath.

His public question to His accusers made them look terribly foolish: "I ask you, which is lawful on the Sabbath: to do good or to do evil, to save life or to destroy it?" (v. 9). Picture the scene described in verse 10 as Jesus "looked around at them all." Eye to eye. Just waiting for someone to give Him an answer. They were struck dumb. Or maybe dumber. Then He said to the man, "Stretch out your hand." And he did. Right there in front of all those perfect and pious-looking people, the man who all his life had probably hidden his handicap under the sleeve of his garment stretched forth his humiliating infirmity—and was healed. It was enough to make those who were sitting by to be "filled with rage," off to their own little corners to discuss "what they might do to Jesus" (v. 11).

It's a question we must answer every time we hear or read a message from His Word. What will we do with Jesus? Will we sit under His teaching? Or just sit by?

What are some practical ways to engage yourself in hearing and reading God's Word?

Setting time aside daily to read his word. Get good rest before Church and go w/ an open heart to God.

PRAYING GOD'S WORD TODAY

Lord, I pray for the boldness of Peter and John who, knowing the threats being leveled against them, asked that You would grant them the power to speak Your message with boldness, while You stretched out Your hand for healing, signs, and wonders to be performed through the name of Jesus. Shake our assemblies, Lord God, and fill us with Your Holy Spirit, that we might both speak and receive Your message with boldness (Acts 4:29–31).

Lord, I want to speak Your Word and I want to sit under Your word so that I don't go above it and make my own stipulations.

DAY 27

Even God Was Amazed

BEFORE YOU BEGIN
Read Luke 7:1–10

STOP AND CONSIDER

Jesus heard this and was amazed at him, and turning to the crowd following Him,
He said, "I tell you, I have not found so great a faith even in Israel" (v. 9).

Name something that has pleasantly surprised you lately. What makes amazement one of
life's sheerest joys? *Because its something thats*
not expected.

How often do you think God is pleased with what He sees in His people?
I don't think He is really all that
pleased. I know he isn't w/ me.

Jesus almost seems delightfully shocked in this encounter with the centurion, as though He was caught off guard by such faith. I'm so glad God purposed for Christ to know all things yet also to know the thrill of sudden amazement.

Perhaps you've bought into the "wretched worm that I am" mentality enough to be uncomfortable thinking about Christ being impressed by anything wretched man can do. But since we're attempting to develop God's taste in us—to love what He loves, hate what He hates, and marvel at what He finds marvelous—perhaps we could all use a little adjustment in our perception of the divine.

A word God used in Isaiah 66:2 blows my mind. The verse says, "This is the one I esteem: he who is humble and contrite in spirit, and trembles at my word." The word *esteem* means to "regard with pleasure, . . . have respect." God is clearly saying that He respects certain people.

Our difficulty imagining that God could have respect for a mortal is because we confuse attitudes of respect with feelings of inferiority. We tend to view respect as a feeling we have for those we perceive as being superior to us. And on our best day, we are so inferior to Christ that, if not for the Lord's great love (see Lam. 3:22), we would be consumed by holy fire.

If we're to have a balanced perception of all this, however, we must keep in mind that God created us. We are His "workmanship" (Eph. 2:10). He loves us. At times, He actually delights in us. God could have created us void of weakness and with a complete inability to sin. He didn't. He purposely created us with free will and affections so that we could choose Him and love Him in the midst of many options and much opposition.

God didn't create robots. He created humans. So when God sees humans cooperate with His good work and fulfill what they were created to be, He sees something very good. Perfect? No. But respectable? Yes. When the Father sees a human who is prone to selfishness, pride, and arrogance humble himself or herself and tremble at His Word, He esteems that person. Hallelujah! Oh, how I want to be someone God could respect!

Praying God's Word Today

Who, Lord, may ascend into Your presence? Who may stand in Your holy place? The one who has clean hands and a pure heart, who has not set his mind on what is false, and who has not sworn deceitfully. Therefore, we receive Your blessing. We receive righteousness from You, the God of our salvation. Such is the generation of those who seek You, who seek the face of the God of Jacob (Ps. 24:3–6). Lord, I know I have failed You lately and You have been unpleased w/ my actions. I feel that Satan is binding me on ways that I can't express. I want You to be pleased w/ me, but I don't know how. I don't even feel Your Spirit right now or haven't lately. I feel apart from You and I also feel like I am not being fed Spiritually. Help me to find what I need.

DAY 28

Compassion
without Restraint

BEFORE YOU BEGIN
Read Luke 7:11–17

STOP AND CONSIDER
When the Lord saw her, He had compassion on her and said, "Don't cry" (v. 13).

Compassion. Who and what stirs it up in you? What does it look like when it happens?

A hurting soul, a starving child, an abused child, etc.

When you hold compassion back, when you pass by and don't stop to help, what are your reasons for doing so? *Authority because I want to be seen as stern, pride*

How hard must it have been for Christ to possess all authority but stick to a kingdom plan requiring its timely exercise? Even now, He could sneeze on Satan and blow him to oblivion, but that's not the plan. Satan's prompt demise would spare us trouble, but it would also spare us growth resulting in many rewards. So until the right time for Satan's disposal, Christ restrains Himself.

Other areas of restraint must have also been challenging for Jesus as He walked on this pavement. For example, imagine the thoughts this funeral procession must have provoked in the mind of the author of life.

I think the very lordship of Christ overwhelmed Him at that moment in Nain. No one else in the crowd could do anything about the widow's plight. They possessed no power. Christ was the only one present who had lordship over the living and the dead. His heart went out to her. He felt deeply. He spoke only two words to her: "Don't cry." We've all said those two words to someone who was brokenhearted, but I believe Christ probably meant something a little different.

I don't know about you, but most of the time when I've said to someone, "Don't cry," my heart was saying, "Please stop crying. I can't bear to see you in so much pain!" Usually the words come from one who can't stand to see the hurt because she is powerless to help. Christ, on the other hand, is never helpless. When He said, "Don't cry," He meant, "Not only do I hurt for you, but I'm also going to do something about the cause of your hurt."

Verse 14 records Jesus' initial action: "He went up and touched the coffin." Picture the structure more like a stretcher than our Western concept of a coffin. The body was placed on a board and shrouded with burial linens. Now imagine Christ walking up and touching this burial slate.

The first thing we read after Christ touched the bier is that the ones who were carrying it stood still. They probably stood there bug-eyed. You see, for anyone unnecessary to the interment process to risk touching the dead body was a serious no-no. Jesus was ritually defiling Himself. What they couldn't have realized is that the Son of God could not be defiled no matter what He touched. One day soon He would literally take on the sins of the entire world while still remaining the perfect Lamb without spot or blemish.

We've already seen that Christ did not need to touch to heal. He didn't even need to be present. He seemed to touch because it came natural to Him. I'm anxious to share with you

> I believe what comes most naturally to Christ every time He encounters need is to instantly fix it.

what "touched" means in today's context. The word is *haptomai*, from the word *hapto*, meaning "to connect, bind." *Haptomai* means "to apply oneself to, to touch." The word "refers to such handling of an object as to exert a modifying influence upon it." Christ Jesus literally connected Himself to the situation. We apply all sorts of medication for hurts. Christ took one look at this woman's grief and applied Himself.

I hope you'll also be blessed by the Greek antonym or opposite term for "touched"—*egkrateuomai*. You will find the English translation of this word listed at the very end of the fruits of the Spirit in Galatians 5:22–23. The word is "self-control."

In today's text, imagine Christ acting out of exactly the opposite of self-control. Stick with me here until you grasp the meaning. When Christ saw the woman in such agony and faced with such hopelessness, I'm suggesting He literally cast off self-restraint and *reacted!* The difference between Jesus and us is that He doesn't sin even when He casts off self-control! Christ does not depart from the Spirit whether He responds or reacts.

Herein lies the most profound difference between the miracle in Nain and the previous miracle of the centurion's servant in Capernaum. In the widow's case, the only prerequisite was her pain. Unlike the centurion, she made no request. She exhibited no faith. In fact, we have no idea if the grieving mom even realized Christ existed. She was probably too enveloped in her own agony to notice. He awaited no conditions nor apparently had any intention of using the moment for instructional purposes.

Jesus ran into a woman in hopeless despair and just reacted with what came most naturally to Him—healing mercy. Oh, how I praise Him! I believe we possibly have a small glimpse into what Christ would do in every one of our despairing situations if a greater plan was not at stake. I believe what comes most naturally to Christ every time He encounters need is to instantly fix it. Is it possible He exercises great restraint to work any other way in the face of devastation? I think so.

A plan of profound importance exists that sometimes overrides the miracle we desperately desire. But I am comforted to know that instantaneous healing and resurrection power come even more naturally to our Christ than waiting and working through long but necessary processes. The biggest reason why I can trust in the sovereignty of God is because I am so utterly convinced of the sweetness of God.

How about you? Are you convinced God is sovereign? Are you convinced He is kind, even sweet? Why or why not? _____

_____

_____

_____

_____

_____

_____

_____

Praying God's Word Today

Lord God, when You worked through Elisha to restore life to the son of the Shunemite woman (2 Kings 4:8–37)—just on the other side of the hill from Nain—he had to lay on the boy until the dead body grew warm. But Jesus, You simply spoke and said, "Young man, I tell you, get up!" (Luke 7:14). What a great gulf exists between our power and Yours, between our compassion and Yours. Thank You for bearing such mighty strength on Your shoulders and such deep love in Your heart.

Day 29

Faith and Doubt
inside the Four Walls

BEFORE YOU BEGIN
Read Matthew 11:2–5

STOP AND CONSIDER
When John heard in prison what the Messiah was doing, he sent
a message by his disciples and asked Him, "Are You the One
who is to come, or should we expect someone else?" (vv. 2–3).

Is your life marked by frequent periods of doubt? If so, what are some of the most common
things you find yourself feeling suspicious about? <u>I wonder if my Beliefs</u>
<u>are the right beliefs</u>

What's the most common way that your doubts are alleviated? What thoughts cross your
mind as you feel yourself shaking free from them? <u>When I'm under stress</u>
<u>and have so much time to think. I know</u>
<u>better than to doubt Because I know Jesus</u>
<u>is real because I feel him</u>

People who seem to live out the faith almost flawlessly inspire me; but I am also moved to meditation by those who grapple and wrestle with it. I find that rather than give me "permission" to doubt, their stories usually give me permission to move through my doubt to a place of spacious faith. May God use today's reading toward such an end.

Both Luke and Matthew tell us that John the Baptizer sent messengers to Jesus asking if He was the Messiah. Jesus told them to return to John and tell him just what they had seen: "The blind receive sight, the lame walk, those who have leprosy are cured, the deaf hear, the dead are raised, and the good news is preached to the poor" (Luke 7:22).

Matthew, however, gives us one additional piece of information about the situation. John sent his disciples, all right . . . from his prison cell (Matt. 11:2). Mark 6:17–18 tells us that John was there because he confronted King Herod about his adultery. Do you suppose John's location may have influenced the question he sent his disciples to ask Jesus?

My heart is awash with compassion for a man who sat in prison two thousand years ago. Four walls closing in surely must limit your vision. The facts to support Christ's messiahship were all there. I'm pretty certain John knew it. Furthermore, the baptizer knew Jesus was the Messiah the moment he saw Him at the Jordan River. But time and circumstances can dull the image on your faith perception, and leave you feeling not sure *what* you believe.

I don't think John's sudden bout with doubt had anything to do with public merit. It was a private matter. John had heard the wonders Christ had done for others. I think maybe his faith was shaken because he could have used a wonder for himself, and he didn't appear to be getting it. John knew with his head that Jesus was the Messiah. Sitting in that prison cell, I think he was having a little trouble knowing it with his heart.

We don't have trouble relating here. Have you known Christ long enough to witness His marvelous works? Have you heard testimonies of His intervening power? Even after such evidence, has your faith ever been greatly shaken because of something He didn't do for you personally? Like John, have you ever found yourself waiting and waiting on Christ to come through? Have you ever endured long stretches of suffering on a certain matter while hearing all sorts of wondrous works He was doing elsewhere?

It hurts, doesn't it? We can be believers in Jesus for years, literally seeking Him, finding Him, and serving Him—then suddenly have a staggering bout with doubt. Overwhelmed with guilt and fear, we'll think, "How in the world could I be doubting after all this time?" It's a horrible feeling!

I'd like to suggest, however, that these kinds of doubts are probably not coming from our heads. They're coming from our hearts. Our feelings. Our emotions. Our hurts.

> My heart is awash with compassion for a man who sat in prison two thousand years ago. Four walls closing in can limit your vision.

John was not like "a reed swayed by the wind" (Luke 7:24). Rather, he was a man of absolute conviction. That's exactly what faith means. *Pistis*, the Greek word translated "faith," means "firm persuasion, conviction." For our purposes today, "firm persuasion" or "conviction" represents head-faith! Perhaps John had questions, but they weren't enough to sway the reed! If John had truly harbored deeply embedded questions about Christ's authenticity, I don't believe Jesus would have hesitated to rebuke him. He certainly didn't hesitate with some others. Yet Christ was very gentle with John. He simply reminded him that He was fulfilling His job description to the letter.

I believe the root of John's question was, "Why am I sitting in prison while Jesus is going about His business all over the countryside?" Surely John was wondering how he was supposed to "prepare the way" for Him from prison. If Jesus were meeting all the criteria of messiahship, He was supposed to be proclaiming freedom for the prisoners (see Luke 4:18). And John knew a prisoner who could use a little freedom.

John's ministry had lasted only about a year. The baptizer could not have imagined that his purposes had been so quickly fulfilled. John couldn't have foreseen that he was a shooting star leading the way in the night until the dawn would rise.

Our discussion raises an important question: If a real difference exists between head-doubt and heart-doubt, is heart-doubt "no big deal"? When our emotions begin to override what our minds know is true, can we just surrender to our heart-doubts? I don't think so. Our heart-doubts can be very dangerous if we remain in them. But, if we wrestle through them with the Lord Jesus, when we get to the other side of our crisis, we will find ourselves spilled into a place of spacious faith!

How would you describe the difference between "head-doubt" and "heart-doubt"? Which is the most dangerous and hardest to overcome? Who are some people you know who struggle mightily with this, and need your prayer and encouragement? "Head-doubt" is knowing the truth. You belief it and carve it into you mind. But People think with their heart. "Heart-doubt" is going along w/ your emmotions at what time. I believe that "heart-doubt" is the most dangerous because you are going on emmotions and not by what you know.

PRAYING GOD'S WORD TODAY

Lord, I am grateful that Your Word says to have mercy on those who doubt (Jude 22), but also that you admonish us to be people of faith, not like the surging sea, driven and tossed by the wind (James 1:6). I pray, Lord, for Your steadying strength of mind and heart.

Lord, I know that I have had some doubts lately. Doubts about You and about Your will for my life. Remind me of Your wonderous love. Let me set the truth that I know in my head and place it in my heart. Lord, I want to follow You and not doubt Your will for my life. I think I was feeling like John felt, seeing results of You in the lives of others and not seeing them w/ me. Lord, I know You are with me and that You will guide me in the way I should go.

DAY 30

Falling Forward

BEFORE YOU BEGIN

Read Luke 7:23–30

STOP AND CONSIDER

Blessed is the man who does not fall away on account of me (v. 23 NIV).

What are the greatest dangers of doubt? What problems does it cause, both to the doubter and to those who are nearby enough to listen and observe? The greatest danger is falling away from God. It cause those nearby to believe the doubts

What is Jesus' response to doubt in His children? In what ways does He deal with us when we have honest questions? His response is so that those who do not fall away on account of me our blessed. When we have honest answers, He answers us w/ honest truth

It is a real challenge to work through our doubts and not let them imprison us like John's were threatening to imprison him! Christ stated the biggest risk of doubt in verse 23: "Blessed is the man who does not fall away on account of me."

The original word for "blessed" is *makarios*. Revel in this definition of the term: "Biblically, one is pronounced blessed when God is present and involved in his life. The Hand of God is at work directing all his affairs for a divine purpose, and thus, in a sense, such a person lives *coram Deo*, before the face of God."[6] Luke 7:23 tells us these words apply to the person who doesn't fall away on account of Christ.

What does "falling away" mean? The Greek word, *skandalon*, means "a cause of stumbling." Add the meanings of these two definitions and we arrive at the following sum total in Luke 7:23: "The Hand of God is at work directing divine purpose, or blessing, in all the affairs of the one who doesn't let the perceived activity or inactivity of Christ trap him or make him stumble." It's a mouthful, but chew on it awhile!

I don't think Luke 7:23 is talking about falling away from Christ. It's talking about falling over a stumbling block into a trap. One of Satan's most effective devices for causing a devout believer to stumble is to trap him over a matter of faith. Satan even tries to use Christ Himself against us. The most effective faith-trap Satan could set for a Christian is to tempt him or her to doubt the goodness, rightness, or mightiness of Christ.

Note that Christ held John in highest esteem even after being questioned. John was under a terrible strain, and his martyrdom was imminent. Christ knew that! He could handle John's questions because He knew the heart and mind from which they came. After proclaiming that no one born of women was greater than John, Jesus said the "least in the kingdom of God is greater than he" (v. 28).

Please understand that this statement in no way diminished John. Christ simply meant that a new era was unfolding in the kingdom calendar, and to be a part of it would be greater than being a prophet under the old Covenant. Thank God every day that you live this side of Calvary!

Praying God's Word Today

Lord Jesus, I pray that you will continue equipping us to live in a manner worthy of Your gospel—standing firm in one spirit, with one mind, working side by side for the faith, and not being frightened in any way by our opponents. For it has been given to us on Your behalf not only to believe in You but also to suffer for You (Phil. 1:27–29). May we do so with perseverance, humility, and eternal gratitude. As I go through suffering, I tend to doubt you because I have taken my eyes off you and put them on my circumstances. God, I pray that my faith will be strong and as I am going through these times of trials, I will keep my focus on you and clear my mind of all doubts.

DAY 31

At Home in a
Pharisee's House

BEFORE YOU BEGIN
Read Luke 7:36–38

STOP AND CONSIDER
Then one of the Pharisees invited Him to eat with him.
He entered the Pharisee's house and reclined at the table (v. 36).

What types of people would you least enjoy spending an evening with? What is it about them that makes them so hard to be around? Negative people because no matter what you say, they are never happy. Rude because they upset me.

How does a desire to be Christlike affect this feeling of yours? What would be different about your life if every wave of prejudice was silenced? It would make me think before I judge. There is a reason they are this way because something has happened to them. I need to pray for them

Our scene unfolds in the dining area of one of the more prestigious homes in the village. The Pharisee's home was large enough to accommodate Jesus and an undisclosed number of other guests. The Pharisee's wife and any other women involved probably ate separately. They would not have considered this a slight since the men customarily practiced segregated fellowship in many social settings. Incidentally, their manly discussions often turned into passionate theological debates that they thoroughly enjoyed. Such conflict tends to make me nervous, so I would happily have stayed in the kitchen with the dessert and coffee.

Do you have difficulty picturing Christ in this scene? Do you imagine Him never fitting into a Pharisee's home? I think God desires to broaden our understanding and fine-tune some of our mental footage of Christ. The more I study His earthly life, the more I'm grasping that He could fit in anywhere . . . and nowhere.

Remember, Christ is void of all prejudice. He was no more likely to stereotype all Pharisees than He was to stereotype all who were poor, blind, or ill. Furthermore, He was just as anxious to save them from their sins. The obvious difference was how anxious the individual was to be saved.

Before we are too harsh in our view of the Pharisees, we are wise to remember that their negative tendencies resemble those of anyone—even someone in our day and age, someone you could name without thinking twice—who values religion and ritual over relationship with the Savior. Interestingly, in the Gospels not once do we see a Pharisee who is confronted in the stronghold of legalism and self-righteousness ever admit to seeing it in himself. My point is that no one is likely to see him or herself as pharisaical without an honest and courageous look inside. In fact, our story never indicates that Christ's host received the message delivered to him through these events.

But it doesn't mean that Jesus would automatically thumb his nose at an invitation just because of what this man stood for. Jesus is willing to reach into anyone's life, no matter how sinful they are or how sinless they think themselves to be.

PRAYING GOD'S WORD TODAY

Father, I earnestly desire to hold my faith in Christ without showing favoritism, because I know that when I show favoritism, I sin against You and am convicted by the law as a transgressor. Help me, please, to speak and act as those who will be judged by the law of freedom (James 2:1, 9). Father God, I want to change my attitude when I see the way people act. I need to stop judging them on their first impression. I don't know what they have gone through that has caused them to act that way. Help me to speak kind of them even after they are gone. I need to pray for them and have actions that show You.

DAY 32

Talking to Ourselves

Before You Begin
Read Luke 7:39–48

Stop and Consider

When the Pharisee who had invited Him saw this, he said to himself,
"This man, if He were a prophet, would know who and what kind
of woman this is who is touching Him—she's a sinner" (v. 39).

Most of us would be terrified for our thoughts to be heard and broadcast like this. How liberating would it be, though, if we were pure enough inside not to be ashamed? _____

It would be greatly liberating if our thoughts were pure enough to be heard

In very practical terms, what could you do to improve the quality of your thought life?

Spend more time w/ God, then w/ worldly things

I am learning so much in my journey with Christ Jesus—lessons I wish I had learned long ago. I am learning that my heart and mind are of greater importance to Him than my words and deeds. Our innermost places desperately need daily purification. Part of the process is recognizing and confessing judgmental, impure, or critical thoughts before they can make their way to our mouths and our actions. But God really can change our negative thought processes, attitudes, and motives. The process takes time and cooperation, however, because these thought patterns are just as much habitual sin as the transgressions of the woman of ill repute.

We certainly see how deep-seated this tendency is by hearing the Pharisee talking "to himself." This phrase and Christ's response have great importance because they force us to realize that He holds us responsible for the things we say to ourselves. (Ouch.) Yes, He reads our minds. And sometimes, our minds need a viewer rating.

Don't overlook the fact that Christ's willingness to allow the woman to wash His feet caused the Pharisee to question whether or not Jesus was a prophet. The Pharisee implied that Jesus obviously did not know what kind of woman she was. The original wording is quite interesting. The English "what kind" is derived from two Greek words: *poios*, meaning "what," and *dapedon*, meaning "soil." The Pharisee's comment that Christ did not know where she came from literally meant "He has no idea the dirt she comes from."

You know what, beloved? Dirt is dirt, and we've all got it no matter where we come from. I'm not sure Christ sees one kind of dirt as dirtier than another. One thing is for sure: His blood is able to bleach any stain left by any kind of dirt. Oh, thank You, Lord.

I like the King James Version of Christ's first response after He read the Pharisee's thoughts: "Simon, I have somewhat to say unto thee" (v. 40). Lest you think I'm feeling pious in my deep compassion for the habitual sinner, please know I'm presently shuddering over the times Christ has had "somewhat" to say unto me! I also love the King James Version response of the Pharisee: "Master, say on" (v. 40) makes me grin. I wonder what he was expecting the Master to "say on"? I have a feeling it wasn't what Christ said.

Christ told a parable of canceled debts. Two men owed money to a moneylender. One owed much, the other only a little, but neither had the money to pay what he owed, so the moneylender canceled the debts of both. Then Jesus asked Simon to summarize which debtor loved the moneylender most. The answer was obvious, but Simon's words "I suppose" revealed his reluctance to acknowledge it. After Simon pinpointed the one with the bigger debt canceled, Christ said, "You have judged correctly" (v. 43). Interestingly, Simon had been judging throughout the whole ordeal. It was just the first time he had judged correctly.

> He holds us responsible for the things we say to ourselves. (Ouch.) Yes, He reads our minds. And sometimes, our minds need a viewer rating.

Christ then brought the parable to life. He compared the way Simon and the sinful woman had responded to Him. All three times Christ's description of the Pharisee's actions began with the unsettling words, "You did not." How poignant. You see, one of the surest signs of an ancient or modern-day "Pharisee" is a life characterized far more by what he or she does *not* do than what he or she does. "No, Simon. You did not sleep around. You did not take bribes. You did not externalize your depravity. But as well, you did not give Me any water for My feet. You did not give Me a kiss. You did not put oil on My head. You did not see yourself as a sinner, and you did not receive My gift of grace—but she did."

He packs the punch into the living parable in verse 47: "Therefore, I tell you, her many sins have been forgiven—for she loved much. But he who has been forgiven little loves little." Not because that's the way it has to be, but because that's the reality of our human tendency.

A couple of additional truths strike a chord in me. First, I see that Christ never downplayed nor minimized her sin. Human sympathy makes excuses like, "What you did wasn't that bad" or "After all you've been through, no wonder . . . " But Christ never calls sin less

than it is. To picture Christ minimizing the woman's sinful past is to miss the entire point of the encounter. The point is that even though her sins had been many, heinous, and habitual, she had been forgiven, saved, and liberated to love lavishly. Of all the commandments the Pharisee had kept, she (rather than he) had observed the most important one. "Love the Lord your God with all your heart and with all your soul and with all your mind and with all your strength" (Mark 12:30).

The exquisite beauty of loving Christ is that it makes it impossible to keep only one commandment. The Word tells us that the person who truly loves God will pursue the obedient life (see John 14:21) and be far more likely to persevere in trials (see James 1:12). Loving God is the vital lifeline to all the other commandments.

Christ never preached the annihilation of affection. Instead He taught the *redirection* of affection. Human affection first directed to God and filtered through His hands returns to us far healthier and fit for others.

What does it mean to love God "with all your mind"? _To love God w/ all your mind means to focus on things that pure, focus on God_

Praying God's Word Today

O Lord, I want to be wise about what is good, yet innocent about what is evil (Rom. 16:19). I want to wash myself clean from every impurity of the flesh and spirit, making my sanctification complete in the fear of God (2 Cor. 7:1). Yet my life has proven again and again that desire is not enough. Help me, Lord, for I need You desperately.

Lord, I know my mind is not always what is should be. I've been thing on things that shuldn't be and being Negative and thinking on the worst. Help me Lord to love you w/ all my mind.

DAY 33

Go in Peace

BEFORE YOU BEGIN

Read Luke 7:49–50

STOP AND CONSIDER

He said to the woman, "Your faith has saved you. Go in peace" (v. 50).

I don't know what you have been saved from. But I know what I have—and I know what these words say to me: "Go in peace." What do they say to you? *Now that I am saved, I can have a peace that passeth all understanding*

What is Satan perhaps using in your life right now to stop your "going" and to bottle up your "peace"? *My attitude towards work and others. I'm getting frustrated and upset instead of giving everything over to God and allow Him to give me peace.*

During the writing of my book *Breaking Free*, the enemy used every trick in the book to break me. He is our accuser (see Rev. 12:10) and a shameless opportunist (see Luke 4:13). He knew that *Breaking Free* necessitated very deep scrutiny of my history because the study is based on my journey to liberty. My whole life has forever been laid bare before God, but it had never been so vividly laid bare before me. At the taunting of the enemy, I found myself at one point so grieved over the "yuck" in my history that I could not imagine how God could possibly use me. I literally questioned my own calling.

During this painful time, I had a speaking engagement in Louisiana. Customarily someone from the host church delivers a devotional to the team before the conference begins. That day a woman who did not know me, had never heard me speak, had never read a single word I'd written, walked in the door and pulled up a chair in front of me. The entire group could hear her, but the devotional she delivered was for me.

She sat only inches away and never took her eyes off mine. With obvious anointing, she told the story of the sinful woman in the Luke 7 passage, then she said, "I don't know you, Beth. I have no idea why God sent me with such a message to give you, but He told me clearly to say these words to you: 'Tell her that her many sins have been forgiven—for she loved much.'" I cannot describe my feelings then or my feelings now.

This Scripture is the only one framed on my desk. It sits only inches from my computer. As I sit at my desk, I stare at the reminder of God's unreasonable grace, and I'm reminded that I'm forgiven. Indeed, how could someone like me not love Him much?

Perhaps, as it did for me, this passage causes you to picture yourself in this sinful woman's place. If you, too, have been in this scene with Jesus, perhaps you know the inner struggle of a sinful past. Oh, how I would love to be for you today what that woman in Louisiana was to me during that difficult time. Allow me to pull up my chair right in front of you, look you in the eye, and tell you what He told me to say: "Your many sins have been forgiven—for you love much." Go in peace.

PRAYING GOD'S WORD TODAY

I think back to Hannah, Lord, a woman with a broken heart, crying out to Eli who had overheard her wailing prayer, "Don't think of me as a wicked woman; I've been praying from the depth of my anguish and resentment." Eli responded, "Go in peace, and may the God of Israel grant the petition you've requested of Him" (1 Sam. 1:15–17). My petition is that You would help me realize the power and purity of Your indwelling righteousness, for it is the only thing I can rely on—and I know it is more than enough, even for me.

Lord, I need Your peace. I need to focus on You daily and allow You to give me the peace that passeth all understanding. When I'm struggling God, send me that urgent need to pray for that peace

DAY 34

Sowing Lessons

BEFORE YOU BEGIN
Read Luke 8:4–15

STOP AND CONSIDER
He said, "The secrets of the kingdom of God have been given
for you to know, but to the rest it is in parables" (v. 10).

Think of one thing you've learned recently, simply from being in and hearing the Word.

That its okay to be a fool for Jesus

What has Satan done to try snatching it away from you? How has He attempted to make
you doubt it or discount it? He puts doubt in me. makes
me feel embarassed and makes me
think that others are judging me
and laughing at me.

The parable of the sower helps us understand the obstacles that limit us and the elements that would free the Spirit to teach us the deep things of God. But before we look at the differences in each type of "soil," let's address a critical common denominator: all four heard the Word, yet only one produced a harvest.

It is not enough to hear the Word! We have just stumbled on my greatest burden for the body of Christ. How many people sit in church services where Scripture is never taught? They're not even hearing the Word of God! Furthermore, what masses of believers hear the Word but continue to live in defeat because they don't apply it?

I was one of them. I desperately wanted to change. I was miserable in my captivity. I just didn't understand that the power to be transformed was in the authentic application of Scripture. Our obedience is not to make God feel like the boss. Trust me. He's the boss and He knows it. Our obedience to apply the Word of God is so we can live victorious lives that glorify our Father in heaven. Hearing it is simply not enough.

Now let's consider each of the types of soil the seed of God's Word fell on.

1) The seed along the path. Luke 8:12 tells us Satan possesses the ability to come and take away the word from a hearer's heart, although not the *believing* hearer's heart. Once we've received the Word, it's out of his reach. He can try to distort our understanding of it, but he cannot steal it. As we'll soon see, however, we can give it up by our own volition.

The Greek word for "take away" gives the image of an owl swooping down, snatching its prey in its claws, and soaring back victoriously to its perch. Scripture implies countless reasons why Satan desires to snatch the Word from us before we've internalized it. Imagine the evil nature of one who seeks to keep people from being saved.

2) The seed on the rock. The rocky soil doesn't just receive the Word. It receives the Word with joy! How eye-opening to realize that we can hear the Word and receive it joyfully, yet never let it penetrate the depths. Listen, some of the words of God are hard! I think He'd rather see us receive a Word, wrestling over it with tears and letting it take root, than to jump up and down with ecstatic joy for only a while.

The shallow hearer only believes until the "time of testing" (v. 13). What a shame! We miss one of life's most awesome experiences if we don't see God's Word stand up under trial. He wants to show us it works. He wants to show us He works! If we stop believing, we will never know the power and faithfulness of God.

3) The seed that fell among thorns. These hearers are defeated by the distractions of the world: worries, riches, and pleasures. You don't have to be rich to be distracted by riches. You don't have to have much to want more. Working ourselves into the ground to afford more things is symptomatic of this.

> Distraction of all kinds is our biggest challenge in this pursuit. The distracted hearer chokes on his or her own appetites.

The word for "pleasures" is *hedone*, from which we get our term "hedonism." Hedonism views "pleasure, gratification, and enjoyment" as the chief goals of life. Please take caution before you view all forms of pleasure as an enemy of the faithful believer. Few things frustrate me more than people who picture the Christian life as entirely sacrificial and for martyrs only. Walking with Christ is the greatest pleasure of my life. But even this sacred pleasure cannot be my goal. Knowing and pleasing Christ must be my goal. Luke 8:14 says they also don't "mature," which is far more than unfortunate. It's a tragedy. The word "mature" comes from two Greek words: *telos*, meaning "end, goal, perfection," and *phero*, meaning "to bring, bear." The hearers of the Word who are distracted by the constant call of the world will never fulfill God's awesome plan for their lives. According to 1 Corinthians 2:9, distracted individuals miss life's greatest treasure. No mind has even conceived "what God has prepared for those who love Him."

4) The seed on good soil. The good soil represents the one who hears the Word and retains it. "Retains" pictures chewing the Word up and swallowing it until it occupies a place in us. When God's Word is deliberately internalized, it will be authentically externalized because it's no longer what we do—it's part of who we are.

Isaiah 55:11 declares that God's Word will not return void or empty. It will accomplish the purposes for which He sent it. That's a fact. But I want it to accomplish and achieve in me, don't you? When this generation asks who Christ's brothers and sisters are, I want Him to point us out joyfully. For our kinship to be obvious, we've got to hear God's Word and do it. When He sends forth His Word, may He find fertile soil in each of us.

Then, when we've reached our lives' intended goals, we will go out in joy and be led forth in peace, the mountains and hills will burst into song before us, and all the trees of the field will clap their hands. Persevere, doer of the Word. A harvest is coming.

What are some of the key ingredients of fertile "soil"? What few things have kept you most open to retaining, germinating, and bearing fruit with the implanted Word? _____

Retains , Internalized then externalized
Distractions,
my own desires, laziness have kept me
from spending time in the word.

PRAYING GOD'S WORD TODAY

Father, I am encouraged by the example of Isaac, who sowed seed in the land of promise and reaped a hundred times what was sown. You blessed Him, Lord, and he became rich—and kept getting richer until he was very wealthy (Gen. 26:12–13). May Your investment of Your Word in me produce a similar bounty, making me fruitful in all things and a pleasure before Your eyes. Father God, help me to keep my focus on your Word. Continue to give me that desire for your Word so that I may grow in you.

DAY 35

Family Matters

BEFORE YOU BEGIN

Read Luke 8:1–3, 19–21

STOP AND CONSIDER

He replied to them, "My mother and my brothers are
those who hear and do the word of God" (v. 21).

How do you think Mary processed these words of Jesus? How about His brothers?

I think Mary took it to heart and pondered his words
and examined her life. I think it upset His
brothers because @ this time, they did not believe
who He said He was

When Scripture seems offensive to us, when God's way seems harsh and insensitive, what
does that tell us about Him? And what does it tell about us? That means
that we are not living the way we should
be living. I think it shows God's
Compassion because He cares for us so much
and He wants to get across to us what
we have been ~~doing~~ doing wrong.

One of my chief goals in this journey is for us to feel as if our feet have felt the warmth of the sand in every place where Jesus stood. In Luke 8, we have a fresh opportunity to adjust our mental images to include a few new people on the scene. In addition to the Twelve, Jesus had other companions. "Women who had been cured of evil spirits and diseases: Mary (called Magdalene), from whom seven demons had come out; Joanna . . . Susanna, and many others" followed Him (v. 2).

Whether or not these received a verbal invitation the way the Twelve had, a powerful force drew them. After everything Christ had done for them, these women could not help but follow Him. You don't have to talk many freed captives into serving Christ. Like Paul in 2 Corinthians 5:14, the love of Christ compels them.

But it didn't seem to compel some of those who might have seemed most suited to cling to Him—His physical family. When His mother and brothers came to see Him but could not get to Him because of the crowd, Jesus had some strong words for them.

But Jesus was not *rejecting* His family as much as He was *redefining* it. His statement reflected inclusion more than exclusion. Christ's family probably came to take Him home to keep Him from appearing foolish. They surely weren't there to encourage Him. John tells us "even his own brothers did not believe in him" at this time (John 7:5).

Of course, we know that Mary certainly believed Jesus was the Son of God, but the pressure of family members can be quite forceful. Perhaps her other sons were intent on confronting Jesus, and she came along to act as a peacemaker. Sound familiar, moms? You don't have to be a mother to imagine how she felt in her present position.

Christ's revolutionary words that redefined His family dynamics are as critical for us today as they were for those who heard them then. Don't miss the profound importance of God's Word. According to Luke 8:21, our kinship to Jesus Christ is directly revealed through what we do with the Word of God. What you are doing right now—studying His Word—is not just a good idea. It is the very warmth and vitality of the family bloodline—proof that we are family to Jesus Christ.

Praying God's Word Today

O Lord, may we be doers of Your Word and not hearers only, deceiving ourselves. Because if anyone is a hearer of the Word and not a doer, he is like a man looking at his own face in a mirror; for he looks at himself, goes away, and right away forgets what kind of man he was. But the one who looks intently into the perfect law of freedom and perseveres in it, and is not a forgetful hearer but a doer who acts—this person will be blessed in what he does (James 1:22–25). May this be spoken of me as You continue transforming my heart.

Lord, I need to be more of a doer of Your word and not just a hearer. I have been going through a slump lately. I am letting the things of this world get me down instead of coming to You to help me carry these burdens. I'm also letting little stupid things get to me instead of listening to Your Word. God, I want to do better. Help me to never forget to come to You.

DAY 36

You and Whose Army?

Before You Begin

Read Luke 8:26–39

Stop and Consider

When he saw Jesus, he cried out, fell down before Him, and said in a loud voice, "What do You have to do with me, Jesus, You Son of the Most High God" (v. 28).

These accounts of demon possession can be disturbing and confusing, even though they do reveal Christ's delivering power. What questions do they bring to mind in you? _____

_____

_____

We're going to talk about some of the things we can learn from these passages. But before we start, what do you find most encouraging about Christ's victory over demons? _____

_____

_____

_____

After rebuking the waves—and a boatload of disciples—Jesus arrived in the territory of the Gerasenes where they promptly encountered a memorable individual. The man they met was naked, lived among the tombs, possessed superhuman strength, and—did I mention—provided rent-free housing for a legion of demons. This demon-possessed man not only had the power to break ropes and chains; he also supernaturally recognized Jesus as the Son of God. We want to consider several points coming from the encounter.

1) Our God is even God over the godless. The second that Christ stepped His foot on their "turf," the demons knew He carried His authority with Him. As hard as the demonic world tries to keep Him out, no one can keep Christ out of any place He is determined to go. Verse 28 tells us that when the demoniac saw Jesus, he cried out and fell at his feet. While I certainly wouldn't confuse the demoniac's trip to His knees with worship, it definitely was a sign of the demon's acknowledgment that Christ was the Son of the Most High God.

2) The demons may have anticipated Christ's coming. Even my most conservative commentaries entertained the idea that the storm on the way could have been an attempt by the kingdom of darkness to discourage Christ's arrival. We see a hint toward the possibility of this idea in the way Christ rebuked the wind and waters as if they were disobedient. Could they have been temporarily acting under the instruction of the god of the air (see Eph. 2:2)? Just food for thought, but it would help to explain why the demoniac met Christ on the shore, knowing for certain who He was.

3) The demons know their time is limited. Luke focused on only one of the demoniacs, but Matthew tells us that there were actually two. He also tells us that they begged Jesus not to torture them "before the appointed time" (Matt. 8:29). The demons knew something we may sometimes forget. Satan, too, is filled with fury because he knows that "his time is short" (Revelation 12:12)

I don't believe the plan for the Son of God to come to earth was any secret. I believe Satan knew what was going to happen. I just don't think he knew when. Seeing the Word wrapped in flesh reminded him that his time allotment was getting shorter and shorter.

In the same way, the demons controlling the man on the Gerasene shore knew a day of reckoning had been appointed for them.

4) Demons can enact supernatural strength. Matthew tells us that "they were so violent that no one could pass that way" (Matt. 8:28). Luke tells us that the demons enabled the man to break chains (see Luke 8:29). I feel the need to stress something about supernatural power: not all of it comes from God! I have felt chills run down my spine when I've heard someone say: "It had to be God! It was totally supernatural!" At times Satan is able to display signs and wonders. But remember, ours is the Prince of Peace. All conflict He ordains is for the ultimate purpose of peace under His righteous rule. Oh, for the government that will be on His shoulders! (see Isa. 9:6–7).

> Our God is even God over the godless. The second that Christ stepped His foot on their "turf," the demons knew He carried His authority with Him.

5) Solitary places can be used by God or Satan. This man "had been driven by the demon into solitary places" (v. 29). Jesus also valued solitary places. In Mark 6:31, He said to the disciples, "Come with me by yourselves to a quiet place and get some rest." We all need times of solitude to spend with God. But our times of isolation can be used by the enemy as well. If we isolate ourselves from the support of others, Satan can have a field day.

Only Christ can defeat demonic powers. Without Christ, a "legion" of humans cannot take authority over a single demon. However, Jesus the One and Only can instantly take authority over legions of demons. The climactic point of the story reveals an almost laughable irony. The demons begged to be cast into the swine rather than into the abyss. (If you think I'm going to say a word about deviled ham, you're mistaken!)

The villagers came out of the woodwork only to find the talk of the region sitting at Jesus' feet, dressed and in his right mind. The people allowed fear to eclipse the life-

changing facts, and they begged Jesus to leave. He could have healed them, saved them, taught them, sanctified them, and, for heaven's sake, delighted them. But all they wanted Him to do was to leave them.

Jesus left the Gerasenes, all right. But not without a vivid reminder of who He was and what He could do. Long after they recovered from the swine-at-sea incident, there would still be a man about town with a restored mind and real dignity who couldn't seem to hush. Christ told him, "Return home and tell how much God has done for you" (v. 39). How long do you think it had been since he had been home? Not back to the tombs, but home. Clothes on his back. Roof over his head. Soundness in his mind. A message on his tongue. So the man went and told all over town how much Jesus had done for him. All the demons in the air couldn't stop him, for his knees had bowed to a new authority.

Have you ever been afraid of Christ's presence in your life, the way these citizens were? What causes us to fear His nearness? _____

_____

_____

_____

_____

_____

_____

_____

Praying God's Word Today

Truly, Lord, even the winds and the waves obey You (Luke 8:25). I know that You can do anything, and no plan of Yours can be thwarted. I had heard rumors about You, but now my eyes have seen You. Therefore I take back any words of doubt or unbelief, and repent in dust and ashes (Job 42:1, 5–6). You are indeed the Son of the Most High God!

DAY 37

Desperation

BEFORE YOU BEGIN
Read Luke 8:40–42a, 49–56

STOP AND CONSIDER

Just then, a man named Jairus came. He was a leader of the synagogue.
He fell down at Jesus' feet and pleaded with Him to come to his house (v. 41).

When have you been desperate for Jesus' help? What has the power to bring you to your knees, pleading? _____

_____

_____

How do you feel when you approach Him with a deep, pressing, please-do-something-now need? Welcome? Unworthy? A bother? _____

_____

_____

_____

I long to sit at Jesus' feet in heaven and hear Him describe personally His earthly experience. I want to hear all the missing details. I want to hear what He was thinking when certain things happened. And when I do, I think He'll have plenty to say about the text we're observing today.

Upon Jesus' return from across the lake, a crowd greeted Him. Luke 8:40 says they were all expecting Him. (I do dearly love surprise encounters with Jesus, but I think He is quite pleased when we live our lives in expectancy.) Verse 41, however, introduces us to a major player who didn't come just to welcome Jesus. He came *desperate* for Jesus. Jairus was a ruler of the synagogue, but this day no ritual dignity stood in his way. His daughter lay dying, and he threw himself at the feet of Jesus pleading for her life.

Jim Cymbala, in his book *Fresh Wind, Fresh Fire,* wrote, "I discovered an astonishing truth: God is attracted to weakness. He can't resist those who humbly and honestly admit how desperately they need him."[7] This certainly described Jairus on this day. Jairus also reminds me of the centurion in Luke 7. He seemed to understand the concept of authority because of his authoritative position. He seemed to grasp that one ruler existed before whom all others should bow, even if one of those "others" was a ruler of the synagogue.

If you were to ask any set of parents how much they focus on their child when he or she is sick or in some kind of serious danger or distress, they'd tell you they can hardly focus on anything else. This was certainly the case with Jairus. Jesus was his last hope. Who else could heal his little girl from the throes of death?

Whom do you know that is possibly down to his or her very last hope? Perhaps, like me, you even know several. Think of these people and keep them in your peripheral vision today, as well as tomorrow when we look at the story this passage is sandwiched around— Jesus' healing of a woman who had been bleeding for twelve years. He is there for the desperate. He specializes in the hopeless. Every time you think of those who are suffering, think of Jesus, who knows the path through dire need.

PRAYING GOD'S WORD TODAY

Lord, I pray for those today who would say with David, "God, deliver me. Hurry to help me, Lord. I am afflicted and needy; hurry to me, God. You are my help and my deliverer; Lord, do not delay" (Ps. 70:1, 5). I bring them before You by name and need . . .

DAY 38

More than Enough

Before You Begin
Read Luke 8:42b–48

Stop and Consider
In the presence of all the people, she declared the reason she
had touched Him and how she was instantly cured (v. 47).

Describe what makes the lessons learned during long seasons of chronic difficulty unique from those that are learned in emergency situations. _____

_____

_____

Compare the difference between those who suffer bitterly and those who suffer well.

_____

_____

_____

_____

We read in verse 42 that the crowd pressed so closely to Jesus they were almost crushing Him. Yet a woman behind Him touched only the edge of His cloak, and He discerned the difference. Please keep in mind, she never even touched His skin. Amazing! Notice, too, that when Christ asked, "Who touched me?" they all denied it. Odd, isn't it? The people were so close they were nearly crushing Him, but no one admitted to touching Him. Their response reminds me of children too afraid of getting into trouble to admit to something. Did they not realize He wanted few things more than for them to reach out to Him?

When the woman realized she could not go unnoticed, she "came trembling and fell at his feet" (v. 47). Beloved, no one goes unnoticed by Christ—least of all a person acting on faith. I love the fact that the woman came trembling, even though she had exercised enough faith to draw forth the healing power of Jesus. It's good to know that the faithful still come trembling. In fact, their reverence is a critical part of their faith. The truly believing will most certainly also be the bowing.

Why do you think Christ asked her to identify herself? I think one reason might have been so that she could enjoy the healing she had received. Most modern Bible translations don't record one phrase found in the King James Version of verse 48: "Daughter, *be of good comfort:* thy faith hath made thee whole; go in peace." In this way I believe Christ was saying, "Do not go forth as someone who feels like they have stolen a gift! Be of good cheer! I freely give it to you!"

Verse 42 also tells us Jesus was on His way to heal the dying child of Jairus when the woman in the crowd touched the edge of His cloak. Christ Himself described what happened: "Someone touched me; I know that power has gone out from me" (v. 46). The primary point I want to make is that Christ released enough power to heal a woman of a twelve-year hemorrhage, but still had plenty to raise Jairus's daughter from the dead! Let that sink in! I know that you know it with your head, but I want you to receive it in your heart. Christ's power supply is limitless. He's not the Wizard of Oz with a limited number of wishes to grant. His power and mercy are infinite. He can take you much farther than Kansas, Dorothy.

One night at Bible study, I asked the entire group to come to their feet for a time of intercessory prayer. I then asked anyone with an "overwhelming need" that seemed absolutely "insurmountable" to sit down. I don't mind telling you, few people were left standing. And based on their tears, I don't think they were just being dramatic. I had anticipated having enough intercessors left standing to lay hands on all those who sat down. Boy, was I mistaken! For a split second I didn't know how to proceed. Then the Spirit of God seemed to speak to my heart. What joy flooded my soul that very moment as God called upon me to come boldly before His throne and ask for a miracle for every life because He had plenty of power to go around. That's exactly what I did. The testimonies written to me the next week were unforgettable. Virtually everyone witnessed some type of wonder that week.

> When Christ asked, "Who touched me?" they all denied it. Did they not realize He wanted few things more than for them to reach out to Him?

Now hear this: Jesus has more than enough power! Does He seem to be on His way to another need, one that you perceive may be more important than yours? More a matter of life and death? No problem! Reach out and grab that hem! You are not going unnoticed—not even if He's on His way to raise the dead!

Oh, friend, would you dare to believe that He is completely able? If He doesn't grant you what you ask in faith, it is never because He lacks the power. I believe it's because He wants to release an all-surpassing power and reveal an even greater glory through another answer. Will we laugh at the thought like the foolish mourners outside Jairus's home? Or will we be invited into the house to behold a miracle?

I'm giving you more room than usual, beloved, because I want you to identify your greatest need, the deepest desire of your heart. Write it down. Two or three? Write them all. Don't tell me how trivial they seem in comparison to what others are facing! Write them! Then after you've written them all, I want you to consider your list carefully. Now I want you to say out loud: "Jesus, You have enough power."

JESUS

Praying God's Word Today

Lord Jesus, I marvel at stories about those who, like John, could testify to having seen You with their eyes, observed, and touched You with their hands—the Word of life—and who now testify and declare to us also what they have seen and heard (1 John 1:1, 3). Today, I reach out to You myself, so grateful for the privilege of having fellowship with the Father and with His Son Jesus Christ.

DAY 39

Called to What?
Or Called to Who?

Before You Begin
Read Luke 9:1–6

Stop and Consider
So they went out and traveled from village to village,
proclaiming the good news and healing everywhere (v. 6).

What kinds of emotions do you think the disciples experienced after Christ told them what He was equipping them to do? _____

_____

_____

What have you felt Him calling you to lately? How are you responding to this? What are your biggest questions as you grapple to discern His voice and will? _____

_____

_____

I find it interesting that Christ's instruction to His disciples to go and minister was for a specific mission or task. I believe the concepts of calling and task are often confused in the body of Christ. I know that I confused the concepts in the early years of my surrender to ministry.

When I was in my mid-twenties, my wonderful ministry mentor, Marge Caldwell, helped me to see that God had equipped me with some of the speaking gifts. Once I began to exercise those gifts, I assumed that speaking was my calling. God soon made very clear, however, that my calling was to surrender my life every day to His will, to be His woman, and to do what He asked, whatever that was. I remember sensing Him speak to my heart saying, "Beth, I do not want you surrendered to an assignment. I want you surrendered to Me." I realized that God did not want me "hung up" on the kind of assignment He would give me. He didn't want it to matter to me whether He asked me to teach the Word of God to a hundred people or to rock one baby in the church nursery. My calling was to be abandoned to Him.

The Twelve were called to be Christ's learners or pupils. They also were designated apostles, meaning they would be sent forth. What would His pupils be sent forth to do? Whatever He told them. In our human need for the security of sameness, we tend to want one job assignment from God that we can do for the rest of our lives. He's far more creative than that!

You may ask, "Isn't it possible for God to assign a lifelong task such as preaching at one church for forty years?" Absolutely! But we are wise not to make assumptions by surrendering to the assignment! Our calling is to surrender to God. Think of the pitfalls we could avoid if we were more abandoned to God than to a particular kind of service.

Remember the meaning of *disciple*: pupil, learner! We can't keep skipping class—our time with God in the Scripture and in prayer—and expect to know when He's scheduled a field trip!

Praying God's Word Today

Lord, what we will be has not yet been completely revealed to us, but we know that we are Your children! And we know that when You appear, we will be like You, because we will see You as You really are. With this hope in us, we purify ourselves just as You are pure (1 John 3:2–3), and we make ourselves ready for You to employ us in Your service . . . in whatever way You choose to use us.

DAY 40

You Want Us to What?

BEFORE YOU BEGIN
Read Matthew 10:5–10

STOP AND CONSIDER
You have received free of charge; give free of charge (v. 8).

What are some ministries and blessings you wish you could share with others a little more freely than you do now, or at least more freely than you have in the past? _____

_____

_____

What tends to bottle up the freedom of our generosity with others? What do we routinely stumble over in our efforts to be Christ's disciples and servants in the world? _____

_____

_____

_____

_____

Up until now, the Twelve had watched Christ at work and had witnessed His miracles, but they had not yet been empowered to exercise those wonders. I don't imagine the disciples expected to do anything but watch. But they were about to receive a very special welcome to the wild world of Jesus Christ. Jesus called the disciples together and gave them "power and authority to drive out all demons and to cure diseases" (Luke 9:1). Then He sent them out to preach and heal. He told them to take along no provisions but to stay where the people welcomed them.

Wouldn't you love to have eavesdropped on the conversations between the disciples as they prepared to go out? Like us, I'm not sure they had a clue what they had been given. They had the privilege to be the closest earthly companions to the Son of God. They were chosen to witness the most remarkable phenomenon in all human history: the Word made flesh and dwelling among us. They broke bread with Him, laughed with Him, and talked Scripture with Him. They knew the sound of His breathing when He slept. They knew His favorite foods. They watched Him heal the sick, deliver the demon-possessed, and raise the dead. If they had never received another thing, they had been granted a privilege beyond all others. But Christ didn't stop there. He also gave them power and authority.

Christ's words in Matthew 10:8 should inspire us to pour out our lives like drink offerings for the rest of our days. "Heal the sick, raise the dead, cleanse those who have leprosy, drive out demons. Freely you have received, freely give." The word for "freely" is *dorean*, meaning "freely, gratis, as a free gift." I think you might be very interested to see another way this same Greek word is translated into English.

In John 15:25 Jesus said, "They hated me without reason." The phrase "for no reason" is translated from the same word, *dorean*. What does that tell you about the things we've received from Christ? Unreasonable grace! Nothing is reasonable about the love of God or the gifts He so freely gives! Like me, I know you've received freely from God in ways you can't begin to count, but has that unreasonable grace caused you to freely give of yourself to others recently?

Praying God's Word Today

Lord, I know we have not received the spirit of the world but Your Spirit, in order that we may know what You have freely given us in Christ. I pray that we will also speak these things, not in words taught by human wisdom, but in those taught by Your Spirit (1 Cor. 2:12–13). We desire to give freely, Lord, out of the abundance we have received. _____

_____

_____

_____

_____

_____

_____

_____

_____

_____

_____

_____

_____

_____

_____

DAY 41

Dinner on the Grounds

BEFORE YOU BEGIN
Read Luke 9:10–17

STOP AND CONSIDER
"We have no more than five loaves and two fish," they said,
"unless we go and buy food for all these people" (v. 13).

What have been some of your "unless" responses lately—those short-sighted answers that
seem to be the only way God can pull your problem out of the fire? _____

_____

_____

When was the last time you went ahead and took an "unless" action, only to find out later
that if you'd have only waited, God had another "unless" in mind? _____

_____

_____

_____

Any of us who have ever been exhausted by an intense time of ministry can deeply appreciate the opening scene in Luke 9:10. The apostles returned from their preaching and healing mission. Mark pictures the Twelve gathered around Jesus reporting all they had done and taught. What affection floods this setting! We can assume He omnisciently knew everything they had done and taught, yet I love how He celebrated their news with the same excitement as someone at a surprise party.

Sometimes I'll be busy telling God every detail of something exciting that happened, a thousand words a minute, when suddenly I will stop and say, "But I guess You already knew that." Every single time I sense Him saying, "Don't let that stop you, child! Tell on!" Beloved, I so much hope that you feel free to talk to Him with the excitement of a friend.

But Christ not only sees our excitement, He sees our exhaustion. I love the way the King James Version says it: "They had no leisure so much as to eat" (Mark 6:31). He saw their need for leisure over a refreshing meal. His invitation to them is so warm and intimate that my affection for Him swells every time I read it: "Come with me by yourselves to a quiet place and get some rest."

Wouldn't you know it? In the middle of their private getaway, the public showed up. Yet Christ's response to the crowd touches me: "He welcomed them" (Luke 9:11); "They were like sheep without a shepherd" (Mark 6:34). Desperate, vulnerable, without direction, without protection, and He had compassion on them. According to Matthew 14:21, we are safe to picture at least ten thousand people gathering all over the countryside. Christ "healed those who needed healing" (Luke 9:11). The day wore on, and the sun rested again on a western hill. Then about that time, some interesting things began to happen. Consider the following observations with me:

1) Christ sometimes provokes a question so that He can be the answer. I love how John's version tells us Christ prompted the question to Philip, "Where shall we buy bread for these people to eat?" (John 6:5). Verse 6 tells us, "He asked this only to test him." I think Christ might have been testing His disciples to surface what they had learned or, like me,

what they had *yet* to learn! Think of the miracles they had seen Christ perform by this time. Yet they couldn't imagine how they were going to feed all these hungry people. I think Jesus may have been testing them to see if they were beginning to think in a "faith mode." Their response proved they still practiced fragmented faith. While they had seen Christ cast out demons and heal the sick, it had not yet occurred to them He could feed the masses. They still had much to learn about Christ's complete jurisdiction. He can meet our spiritual needs, our emotional needs, and our physical needs. He is both deeply spiritual and entirely practical. Christ was teaching them to see Him, His power, and His authority in every area of life.

> Think bigger, boys! For one day you'll see Me in My glory, then you'll say to me . . . "We should have thought bigger."

2) Christ wants us to be open to what He can do through us. I love the way He tossed the responsibility for feeding the crowd right into His disciples' laps. "You give them something to eat" (Luke 9:13). Mind you, they had received power and authority to heal the sick and cast out demons, yet they looked helplessly at two fish and five loaves as the totality of their resources.

I believe Christ was saying, "Think bigger, boys!"—not only about what *He* could do, but also what *they* could do *in His name*. Where the disciples were concerned, I believe this event was all about stretching their thinking. His words are entirely absent of rebuke. Don't miss the fact that He used the disciples to distribute the meal. He wanted them to feel the weight of the baskets and see the hands of those reaching to be fed. Real power. In real forms. In real life.

3) Christ can perform astounding wonders when we bring Him all we have. Matthew 14:17 records the disciples saying, "We have here only five loaves of bread and two fish." Christ responded, "Bring them here to me." Beloved, I want you to hear something loud and clear: no matter what your "only" is, when you bring all of your "only" to Jesus, it's huge!

When we bring Him everything we have, He multiplies it beyond our wildest imagination. On the other hand, we can surrender Him "some" of our lot, and it can dwindle to virtually nothing.

4) Christ saved a basket-load of leftovers for each disciple. The disciples picked up twelve baskets of leftovers. I just can't make myself think that was a coincidence. I'm no mathematician, but the numbers work for me. The people were fed. The disciples each wound up with a basketful of leftovers. That's what happens when you take part in God's provision.

Think bigger! You choose the issue that's pressing on you right now—the one that seems impossible to solve or work your way out of. How different might it look if you knew your problem had a "bigger" answer, a "bigger" reason for being there? _____

_____

_____

_____

_____

_____

_____

_____

Praying God's Word Today

Lord Jesus, You have said in Your Word, "Whoever has, more will be given to him, and he will have more than enough. But whoever does not have, even what he has will be taken away from him" (Matt. 13:12). I don't have much, but I want You to have it all. I don't want my "some" to become nothing that You can use. _____

_____

_____

_____

_____

_____

_____

_____

_____

_____

_____

_____

_____

_____

_____

_____

_____

DAY 42

Leftovers
You'll Actually Like

Before You Begin
Read Matthew 14:19–21

Stop and Consider

Everyone ate and was filled. Then they picked up 12 baskets full of leftover pieces (v. 20).

If you're not sensing the approval of God today, would you do some honest soul-searching to see if there's anything that's keeping your fellowship strained and distant? _____

_____

_____

What would you do if you knew God was smiling on you today? How would it change everything? _____

_____

_____

_____

_____

I just have to share another thought with you about this astounding miracle of Jesus, this feeding of the five thousand with His disciples' mere fishes and loaves.

At the age of twenty, my older daughter was asked to speak to a group of teenage girls in Oklahoma. Of my two children she is the shy one. With horror on her face, she told me she was certain God was telling her to say yes. I cannot express to you how far outside her comfort zone this was at the time.

The butterflies never left her stomach from the time of the invitation until the day of the conference. What emotion flooded my heart as I put her on that plane to go speak—instead of the other way around. Contrary to her worst fears, she lived through it! And the young women received a sound message from the Word . . . even if the voice was a little shaky here and there.

The next morning she called me with such a tender heart, her voice cracking, and said, "Mom, I just had my time with the Lord . . . and He was so . . . sweet."

I knew exactly what she was talking about. I said, "Oh, my precious child, you have just experienced that which would be worth selling all your earthly possessions to gain, and yet it's a gift of grace: divine approval. The smiling nod of God. Nothing like it."

With the slightest whisper, my very humble, gentle child said, "Yes."

I'm fighting back tears at the thought. You see, this act of obedience was terribly difficult for her. She could have provided a list of other students, but she didn't. In effect she said, "All I have is this pitiful handful of fish and loaves," and Jesus said, "Bring them to me." When all was said and done, she wasn't sure what the girls had received, but God had given her bread from His Word and she had distributed it the best she knew how.

Amanda was glad to have survived . . . but imagine her surprise when she didn't just survive. The next morning as she sat before the Lord, He handed her a basketful of leftovers. She had been willing to be a disciple. A learner. A novice. He would not have dreamed of leaving her empty-handed.

You either, my friend. It's not His style.

Praying God's Word Today

Father, You have multiplied Your grace and peace to us through the knowledge of You and of Jesus our Lord. For Your divine power has given us everything required for life and godliness. By Your own glory and goodness, You have given us very great and precious promises, so that through them we may share in Your divine nature, escaping the corruption that is in the world because of evil desires (2 Pet. 1:2–4). Hallelujah, praise the Lamb! _____

_____

_____

_____

_____

_____

_____

_____

_____

_____

_____

DAY 43

Hot and Cold

Before You Begin
Read Matthew 16:13–23

Stop and Consider
Peter took Him aside and began to rebuke Him,
"Oh no, Lord! This will never happen to You" (v. 22).

What are some things about Jesus' teaching that you sometimes find very, very difficult to swallow? How have you reacted to these things throughout your life with Him? _____

_____

_____

Why did Jesus choose for His way to be frequently offensive to our natural inclinations?

_____

_____

_____

_____

Try to picture Peter saying something like, "Jesus, can I see You just a minute right over here? Excuse me, brothers. We'll be right back," then commencing his rebuke of the "Son of the living God." In my opinion, Peter the rock was pretty fortunate he didn't get thrown into the nearest lake! A couple of thoughts surface as I look at this interchange:

1) One minute we can be so "on target" and the next minute so "off." Without a doubt, some of my better moments preceded my worst disasters. How about you? I mean, one moment Peter made a statement that Christ said could only have been revealed to him by the Father. The next thing we know he's made a statement Christ attributed to the devil. One minute a rock—the next minute a stumbling block. Whew! What a frightening thought! How on guard we must be.

I keep looking at Peter's words: "This shall never happen to you!" (Matt. 16:22). I wonder, based on Christ's response to him, if in Peter's heart he might have been thinking: "This shall never happen to *me!* I've given up everything to follow You! You can't go dying on us here! We've got a kingdom to build!" Peter didn't understand that Christ's suffering and death were the means by which He would indeed secure the kingdom.

2) All Satan needs to have momentary victory over a disciple is for us to have in mind the things of men. Satan doesn't have to get us blatantly thinking satanic thoughts to have victory over us. All he needs is to get us looking at life from man's perspective rather than God's. But if we surrender our minds to the things of God, we are safe! We don't have to constantly look out for our own best interests, because *He's* constantly looking out for them. What Peter didn't understand is that what may have seemed best in the short run would have been disastrous in the long run. Had Jesus saved His disciples the anxiety of His betrayal, trials, and death, He wouldn't have saved them at all.

On this earth I don't know that we will ever perpetually have in mind the things of God rather than the things of man. But if we don't make the deliberate choice to have in mind the things of God when faced with our biggest challenges, most of us will probably default back to our natural instinct—the things of man.

PRAYING GOD'S WORD TODAY

O Lord, You have warned us in Your Word, "Whoever thinks he stands must be careful not to fall" (1 Cor. 10:12). Help me remember that my ways will always lead me toward danger and death, but Your ways will lead to life and peace. Truly, as heaven is higher than the earth, so are Your ways higher than our ways and Your thoughts than our thoughts (Isa. 55:9).

DAY 44

Daily Denial

Before You Begin
Read Luke 9:23–27

Stop and Consider

He said to them all, "If anyone wants to come with Me,
he must deny himself, take up his cross daily, and follow Me" (v. 23).

What are some of the "daily" things in your life that need to be denied—over and over again—if you're going to be able to follow Christ? _____

_____

_____

Why does He require such "daily" obedience? What would be different about Christianity if all we were asked to do was to "set it and forget it"? _____

_____

_____

_____

Don't miss the fact that Peter was invited to "follow" Jesus even after the horrible *faux pas* of rebuking His Master. I am intrigued that Peter actually heard this invitation three times before Christ ascended to the right hand of the Father: once in Matthew 4:19, again in this passage, and finally in John 21:19. It's almost as if he were getting a crash course in Follow 101, Follow 202, and Follow 303. The first one was to follow Him as a *disciple*. The second one was to follow Him with a *cross*. The third one was to follow Him to *death*. Not coincidentally, tradition teaches that Peter indeed ended up following Christ to the death . . . on a cross.

In Christ's invitation I see two key concepts: *denying self* and *taking up the cross daily*. Those who accept this invitation are called to deny themselves. I don't believe Christ was talking about the things we typically consider self-denial. The issue here wasn't fasting from food, nor was it denying self a single extra. It wasn't about self-loathing either, because Christ commanded us to love our neighbor as ourselves. I believe the primary issue involved in this kind of self-denial is denying our right to be our own authority.

This passage brings us to the sobering realization that what we might think of as being under our own authority—having in mind the things of men—could easily be transferred to Satan's authority. I've learned the hard way that denying my right to be my own boss is what keeps me from getting slaughtered by Satan in warfare. Let's face it: this "be-your-own-boss" stuff is nothing but a myth.

But the second concept is just as vital: the key to true "follow-ship" with Christ is the recommitment to take up the cross daily. One reason I am drawn to Luke's version of this invitation over Matthew's is because he includes that all-important word—*daily*.

In my opinion, Dr. Luke wrote the prescription for the victorious life, and he wrote it for all of us who would desire to become Christ's disciple: live life one surrendered day at a time. Eyes to the East. Hands to the cross. Feet to the path.

PRAYING GOD'S WORD TODAY

Lord God, it is written in Your Word, "Because of You we are being put to death all day long; we are counted as sheep to be slaughtered." And yet in all these things, we are more than victorious through You, the One who loves us (Rom. 8:36–37). Losing to gain. Thank You that none of our sacrifices are truly sacrificial when seen against the abundance of Your grace and sovereignty. _____

_____

_____

_____

_____

_____

_____

_____

_____

_____

_____

_____

_____

_____

DAY 45

Who Is This Man?

Before You Begin

Read Luke 9:28–36

Stop and Consider

Peter and those who were with him were in a deep sleep,
and when they became fully awake, they saw His glory (v. 32).

Why would Jesus choose a mountain as the ideal spot for Him to reveal His glory to His
closest friends? _____

_____

_____

At what points and places in your life has He made His glory known to you . . . in ways
that were indescribably real and unforgettable? _____

_____

_____

_____

God has often chosen to unveil His glory on the top of a mountain. In Exodus, He beckoned His servant Moses to climb the mount and see His glory. Elijah also had a mountaintop view of the greatness of God. So when Christ summoned Peter, James, and John to the top of a certain mountain, there was precedent for it, yet they could never have imagined what awaited them. I think we can rest assured, though, that it was worth the climb.

They saw His glory!

When was the last time you saw Christ transfigured before you? We grow comfortable with the Christ we know. Then suddenly He shatters the box we've put Him in, leaving us asking, "Who is this man?" Christ reserves the right to bring us to places that force us to ask that question again. At those times, if we're willing, Christ will show us a glimpse of His glory, and we will be changed as He transfigures Himself before us.

Jesus regularly seeks to readjust our vision of Him. And I believe the more we are willing to receive from Him, the more He is willing to reveal to us. I think the reason Jesus took Peter, James, and John to the mountain was because they were willing to receive greater revelation. How blessed we truly are when we have eyes that are willing to see and ears that are willing to hear. In the words of Jesus: "Whoever has will be given more, and he will have an abundance. Whoever does not have, even what he has will be taken from him" (Matt. 13:12).

How blessed we are when we want to see Him. How blessed we are when we begin to make our chief cry to Him, "Lord, I want to know You. I want to know the reality of You. I want to know who You really are. Shatter my present perspective and show me the reality of You."

We are a direct by-product of who we believe and who we see Christ to be. I believe He blesses the prayer, "Father, daily show me the reality, the greater reality of Your Son Jesus Christ. Transfigure Him before my very eyes, and then give me the courage to adjust my life to what I see."

PRAYING GOD'S WORD TODAY

O Lord my God, You are very great, clothed with majesty and splendor. You wrap Yourself in light as if it were a robe, spreading out the sky like a canopy, laying the beams of Your palace on the waters above, making the clouds Your chariot, walking on the wings of the wind, and making the wind Your messengers, flames of fire Your servants (Ps. 104:1–4). O my soul, praise the Lord! _____

_____

_____

_____

_____

_____

_____

_____

_____

_____

_____

_____

_____

_____

_____

_____

DAY 46

Assurance of Mystery

Before You Begin
Read Colossians 2:1–7

Stop and Consider
I want their hearts to be encouraged and joined together in love,
so that they may have all the riches of assured understanding,
and have the knowledge of God's mystery—Christ (v. 2).

What are some things you absolutely know about Jesus? _____

_____

_____

But what are some things about Him that are still shrouded in "mystery"? _____

_____

_____

_____

I want you to consider two words for "knowledge" in these verses from Paul's letter to the Colossians. They help us learn something very significant about Christ and about our relationship with Him. The word "knowledge" in verse 2 comes from a wonderful word in the Greek language, *epiginostos*. It means a recognition of who Christ is, with particular emphasis on how this relationship requires participation on the part of the learner. It defines somewhat the security that's found in relationship with Him. Paul is saying, "I want these people to be secure, to have full assurance in their knowledge of Christ."

Now let me point you to the *second* word for "knowledge," which appears in verse 3: "Christ, in whom are hidden all the treasures of wisdom and knowledge." *This* word for "knowledge" is a different word entirely. It is a word that means "present and fragmentary knowledge." Now hang with me a second, because I think this will thrill you. What Paul is saying is that God is the fullness of all security *and* mystery. He meets all our emotional needs as well as all our mental needs.

Something in each of us just loves a relationship that is both secure and mysterious all at the same time. Let me give you a very personal example:

My relationship with Keith is my most personal earthly relationship. I love knowing that I have security—full assurance—in my relationship with my husband. I believe I can tell you, after many, many years of marriage, that I know this man.

But I remember a time when a friend of mine saw my husband having lunch with another woman. She saw that Keith was fairly affectionate to her. He often touched her in a tender way. He even put his arm around her as they walked out of the restaurant.

Well, this sight troubled my friend. But when I found out from her that she had seen him with another woman, I said, "I want to tell you something. I don't know what the explanation is, but I can tell you right now, it isn't what you're thinking."

How fun it was for me when Keith came in later that day and said, "You know who I had lunch with today? Tina. We had the neatest time together."

(Tina, by the way, is my husband's little sister.)

Now I'm not telling you that something bad could never happen to my marriage. However, I have assurance in him and our relationship. For Keith to cheat on me would be so out of character for him, it would never enter my mind.

In fact, I don't know how in the world I could be this blessed, but I don't think I have lived a day of my married life that my husband hasn't told me at least once—maybe even two or three times—how much he loves me. He'll pick up the phone in the course of a very busy, very difficult day and say, "I love you," even if he only has fifteen seconds and then hangs up the phone without saying good-bye. I know at this point in my life that I have security in my relationship with my husband.

> God is the fullness of all security and mystery. He meets all our emotional needs as well as all our mental needs.

Yet not too long ago, I was sitting in the company of some of our friends, and my husband began telling them a story. I watched his almost childlike face. He was so animated! It was a story about a fish fry he had given for his fraternity in college. (We had gone to the same school together; that's where we met and fell in love.)

In recalling this event, Keith said, "I told them all that I was going to have a big fish fry and that we'd have all the fish we could eat." But he ran out of time before he could go out fishing. So he went to the federal game reserve on that campus—which was very well guarded—and did his fishing there.

Now I realize this was illegal, but it was twenty-two years ago and fortunately the statue of limitations has expired.

I want to tell you something, though. As I was watching Keith reminisce that story, I just fell in love with him all over again. When we got in the car to drive home, I laughed and said, "I've never heard that story before!" It was so cute hearing him tell it.

You know what thrills me? Even after all these years, I am still discovering things about my man. I have security in him—yes—but if I had security and no mystery, that wouldn't be any fun, would it? And if all I had was mystery, where would the security be? But in my husband, I have both security *and* mystery.

That's what the Word of God is telling us we all have in Christ.

Don't you just love how Jesus meets our emotional and mental needs? He said, "You have knowledge of Me with security, with full assurance, in relationship with who I am. But you also have constant mystery as I give You these little fragments of knowledge one at a time to open your eyes to My greatness."

Jesus has taught us so much about Himself. There is so much we can be absolutely sure of. But we will never learn it all while we're here. No matter how often we seek Him, we will always be stunned by His greatness.

What would relationship with Christ be like without security? What would it be like without mystery? How glad are you that He has chosen to give us both? _____

_____

_____

_____

_____

_____

_____

PRAYING GOD'S WORD TODAY

I consider everything to be a loss in view of the surpassing value of knowing You, Jesus, as my Lord (Phil. 3:8). This is eternal life: that I may know You (John 17:3). May You even today surprise me with something I've never known about You before, not so I can gloat or experience some thrill. I just want to know You better and love You more. _____

_____

_____

_____

_____

_____

_____

_____

_____

_____

_____

_____

DAY 47

Out of Your Element

BEFORE YOU BEGIN

Read Mark 7:31–36

STOP AND CONSIDER

They brought to Him a deaf man who also had a speech difficulty, and begged Jesus to lay His hand on him. So He took him away from the crowd privately (vv. 32–33).

Has the Lord ever rearranged your surroundings on you, taking you away from where you've been? A move? A new job? A new circumstance you didn't ask for? _____

_____

_____

What do you think His purpose was in doing that? What was He trying to teach you?

_____

_____

_____

_____

Sometimes when Jesus is about to do something really special in our lives, He will rearrange our surroundings. He will take us out of our element, just as He took this deaf man "away from the crowd" to give him a new perspective on God's glory and power.

This reminds me of a time when our daughter Amanda had begun dating a young man. They were just getting to know one another. It was that exciting stage of dating life when everything about this other person is fresh and new and interesting.

They were walking through a shopping mall together, and he turned to her and said, "I want so much to know you, Amanda. And I want you to know me. I want you to know what I love." He began describing to her how much he enjoyed mountain climbing and camping, just being out in the wild—a whole world away from anything that's the norm of everyday life. He went on and on about what it meant to him to be out in the middle of nowhere and to sense nature all around him.

"I'd say that's my element," he concluded. "What's yours?" She looked around the mall and motioned to the sights, sounds, and stores that enveloped her. "*This* is my element." She was dead serious. When she told me about it later, I had to go to my room, shut the door, and fall on the bed laughing. I thought, "Yep, that's her element, all right. She got it honest. Her mother raised her in it."

It's true. I remember how disappointed I was when I figured out that my spiritual gift wasn't shopping at the mall, as I had originally thought. After becoming a serious believer and trying to recognize what my gifts were, I discovered that "fashion" wasn't even on the list of biblical attributes. My theory was blown.

Instead, the Lord was calling me out of my element, growing in me the spiritual gift of love for the body of Christ. But to do that, He needed me in a new set of surroundings, out where He could show me that even if we speak with the tongues of angels, if we don't have love, we may as well be clanging brass.

Until He has us out of our element—and into His—we will never see His glory. We will always be deaf to what He was trying to say.

Praying God's Word Today

Lord, I pray that You would help me learn to be content in whatever circumstances I am (Phil. 4:12). For if I live at the eastern horizon or settle at the western limits, even there Your hand will lead me; Your right hand will hold on to me (Ps. 139:9–10). ───────

───────────────────────────────────────

───────────────────────────────────────

───────────────────────────────────────

───────────────────────────────────────

───────────────────────────────────────

───────────────────────────────────────

───────────────────────────────────────

───────────────────────────────────────

───────────────────────────────────────

───────────────────────────────────────

───────────────────────────────────────

───────────────────────────────────────

───────────────────────────────────────

───────────────────────────────────────

───────────────────────────────────────

DAY 48

We Tried,
But We Couldn't

Before You Begin
Read Mark 9:14–18

Stop and Consider
I asked Your disciples to drive it out, but they couldn't (v. 18).

When you find yourself unable to accomplish much—spiritually speaking—what do you identify as the usual suspects, the usual reasons why? _____

_____

_____

If you could be as victorious and consistent as you'd like to be, what would you most like to accomplish for the kingdom? _____

_____

_____

_____

_____

We are often empowered to do far more than we exercise. In Luke 9:1 we read that Jesus gave the disciples "power and authority to drive out all demons." Had He taken it back? No, they still possessed the power but were unable to exercise it for some reason. What in the world happened to disable them? Let's explore a couple of possibilities.

1) Their most positive influences were absent. Keep in mind that not only was Christ out of sight, but so were the three leaders of the disciples. In moments like these, we learn where our confidence is. If we have boldness when certain empowered believers are close by, but we lose it in their absence, could it be that we've been sipping out of their power shaker of faith instead of filling our own? We'll never discover our strengths in the power of God if we keep drawing off another's.

2) Their strongest negative influences were present. The presence of the teachers of the law must have been terribly intimidating to these comparatively uneducated men. You and I aren't always surrounded by faith-encouragers either. But we can't afford to wait for all the atmospheric conditions to be right before we act on the power of God. In fact, I think God is teaching us that the worst conditions can often provide the best atmosphere to act in faith. He doesn't want our confidence regulated by our audience. If faith-discouragers can shake our confidence badly enough to disable us, our confidence may be in ourselves instead of God.

I remember a time when a critical letter from a seminary graduate shook my confidence. As I read the list of mistakes she was pointing out, I started thinking, "She's right! What in the world do I think I'm doing? I have no formal theological education. I shouldn't even be doing this!" But God reminded me during the following days that I was exactly right: I *shouldn't* be doing this. This ministry is God's. If my confidence is in myself, I'm in big trouble. God also assured me that I will always make mistakes, but they will serve as reminders to my readers never to think more highly of this teacher than they ought. Only One can be taken at His every word.

PRAYING GOD'S WORD TODAY

Lord, I know we carry the treasure of Your presence in clay jars, in order that whatever power dwells within us will be seen to be Yours, not ours (2 Cor. 4:7). So thank You, Lord Jesus, for choosing to be powerful in us. You were crucified in weakness, but You live by God's power. We also are weak in You, and yet we live by Your power as we serve others in Your name (2 Cor. 13:3–4).

DAY 49

If I Can?

BEFORE YOU BEGIN
Read Mark 9:19–29

STOP AND CONSIDER
May times it has thrown him into fire or water to destroy him.
But if You can do anything, have compassion on us and help us (v. 22).

Few of us would be so bold as to ask Christ to His face "if" He was able to do something.
But how do we say the same thing to Him with our actions and attitudes? _____

_____

_____

What do you think Jesus does with our "if you can" questions? _____

_____

_____

_____

_____

After nearly four decades of knowing Christ, I am only beginning to realize the magnitude of the sin of unbelief. The word "unbelieving" in verse 19 means "not worthy of confidence, untrustworthy." This definition implies that when we are faithless, we are concluding that Christ is not worthy of our confidence, that He is . . . (I can hardly bring myself to write the word) . . . *untrustworthy*. The disciples' unbelief was their willingness to let the temperature of their faith rise and fall according to their surrounding dynamics rather than God's steadfast Word. The characteristic cause of all spiritual failure is lack of faith in God.

But the disciples weren't the only ones having a crisis of faith here. The boy's father had been through a lot watching his son suffer. He frequently feared for his son's life. We can sympathize with the despair he felt. But unfortunately, like many people, he was far more familiar with the power of the devil than the power of the Son of God.

Even in our churches, many are learning more about the power of the devil than the omnipotence of the living God! Like the father in this passage, many do not understand that surrounding dynamics, like the length and depth of defeat, have absolutely no bearing on Christ's ability to perform a miracle. Hear it again: *no bearing*.

Consider the dynamics of length and depth in our text today. We know from the father's response to Jesus' question that his son had suffered since childhood (Mark 9:21). Now, the reason Jesus asked how long the boy had been in his present state wasn't because the answer had a bearing on Christ's ability to free him. He asked the question for the purpose of framing a miracle against the backdrop of hopelessness. Then the father, after stating the hopelessness of the boy's condition, made a statement that probably provokes a host of emotions in each of us: "But if you can do anything, take pity on us and help us" (Mark 9:22). I'd like to break down this phrase into several pieces, then consider Christ's response.

• *"But . . ."* This one little word suggests the tiniest mustard seed of faith in the father—a seed Christ compassionately watered. I am continually moved by Christ's willingness not just to meet us halfway but, like the father of the prodigal, to run the entire distance once

we take the first step in His direction. The Word of God is filled with accounts of hopeless situations followed by that wonderful little word: "but . . ."! Because of His great compassion, sometimes that little whisper is all the invitation Jesus needs to show His power.

> Even in our churches, many are learning more about the power of the devil than the omnipotence of the living God!

• *"If You can."* Christ took exception to the father's use of the word "if," because when an action is consistent with the Word of God, the question is never *if* He can. It may be if He *wills*, but never if He can. When those who have access to Christ experience long-term defeat in their lives, it is often wrapped up in a continued "if You can" mentality. We who know Christ must always answer with a resounding: "Nothing is too hard for Him!"

In at least one way, you and I can't claim the ignorance of the father in this story. We assume he didn't know Christ personally. So Jesus didn't reprove the father the same way He reproved the disciples. Like them, you and I know Christ Jesus as far more than a teacher rumored to possess supernatural power. We call Him Lord. Consider the irony of addressing Him as Master of the universe, then asking Him to come to our aid—if He can. Notice the next words from this distraught dad:

• *"If You can do anything."* Contrast the two words from Mark 9 for a moment: "anything" (v. 22) and "everything" (v. 23). Dear one, Christ can't just do *anything*. Christ can do *everything!* Stop wondering if Christ can do "anything" in your situation, and start believing Him to do "everything" glorious!

Immediately the father exclaimed, "I do believe; help me overcome my unbelief" (v. 24). I can't describe the encouragement this father's honesty has given me through the years. First he cried out, "I do believe!" Then he confessed his unbelief. I believe the father changed his tune because he was looking straight into the face of truth. The closer we get to Jesus, the more difficult it is to stretch the truth.

The wonderful part of the father's exclamation is his realization that, although he lacked faith, he wanted to believe! Then he did exactly what he should have done: he asked for help to overcome his unbelief.

I can't count the times I've imitated this father's actions. In my earlier days with God, I viewed faith as my willingness to make a believing statement with my mouth rather than face the questions of my heart. If only I had understood how Romans 10:10 reverses that order: "For it is with your heart that you believe and are justified, and it is with your mouth that you confess and are saved."

It's time for a dramatic change of approach. If we don't have bold faith, let's start asking boldly for the faith we lack. Imagine the love of a God who says, "It's true that without faith it is impossible to please Me. But I am so anxious to reward you with blessing, I'm even willing to supply the faith you lack. Ask Me, My child! Ask Me for what you lack! I am the only One who can help you overcome your unbelief!"

What do You need His help believing Him for today? _____

_____

_____

_____

_____

_____

_____

Praying God's Word Today

Lord Jesus, I love You, even though I haven't seen You. And though not seeing You now, I choose to believe in You, rejoicing with inexpressible and glorious joy because I know I am receiving the goal of my faith, the salvation of my soul (1 Pet. 1:8–10). Therefore, may I—like Moses—leave my Egypt behind and persevere as one who sees Him who is invisible (Heb. 11:27).

_____

_____

_____

_____

_____

_____

_____

_____

_____

_____

_____

_____

_____

_____

DAY 50

Great Questions

Before You Begin
Read Luke 9:46–48

Stop and Consider

An argument started among them about who would be the greatest of them (v. 46).

Is it a good thing or a bad thing to have a desire for greatness within us? Should we be suspicious of its mere presence? _____

_____

_____

Why does it not seem to be enough for us to achieve success unless we're outdistancing someone else's success? _____

_____

_____

_____

_____

The latter part of Luke 9 contains several seemingly disjointed snapshots of the disciples. First we see Jesus attempting to penetrate their thick skulls with the message of His soon-coming suffering and death. "Listen carefully to what I am about to tell you: The Son of Man is going to be betrayed into the hands of men" (v. 44). Hard to make it much clearer than that, wouldn't you say? But we read that the Twelve didn't understand, and that they were afraid to ask Jesus what He meant. Instead, an argument broke out among them about which of them would be greatest. Can you imagine?

Of course we can. We are not much unlike Christ's original disciples. They thought their argument had been a private matter, but Christ knew their thoughts, just as He does ours. We may never have argued with someone openly about our own greatness, but Christ knows our hearts, as well as the attitudes that inhabit them. He knows our society thrives on ambition. And He knows that if we're not extremely discerning, we will bring these same ambitions into the church. He knows our biggest hindrance to greatness as Christians is our desire to be great.

Don't miss the contrast of Christ and His disciples at this point in His earthly tenure. Christ was on the road to greatness, but His road would take Him through betrayal, rejection, suffering, and death. Philippians 2:6–8 tells us Jesus "did not consider equality with God something to be grasped, but made himself nothing, taking the very nature of a servant, being made in human likeness. . . . He humbled himself and became obedient to death—even death on a cross."

How different this is from our own chosen path to greatness. And yet the Scripture uses Christ's model to urge us not to grow weary and lose heart, since Jesus "endured the cross, scorning its shame" for the "joy set before him" (Heb. 12:2–3). He "tasted death" on our behalf. God the Father chose to "make the author of [our] salvation perfect through suffering" (Heb. 2:9–10).

Don't be confused by the idea that the "author of our salvation" became perfect through suffering. He was always perfect in terms of sinlessness. The word "perfect" in this verse is

teleioo, meaning "to complete, make perfect by reaching the intended goal." Christ reached the goal (our salvation and His exaltation) through suffering. His road to greatness was a rocky one. A painful one. He knew it in advance, and yet He set His face resolutely toward the goal and accomplished it for all time. Simply put, we were worth it to Him.

> We are not much unlike Christ's original disciples. Our biggest hindrance to greatness remains our desire to be great.

And no matter how resistant we may be to this call, our road to true greatness will be the same as His—the highway of humility. At times it too will involve suffering, rejection, betrayal, and, yes, even death—to self. The question becomes, "Is He worth it to us?"

Without a doubt, one of the primary works God has sought to accomplish in me is to help me get over myself. The process has been excruciating and will no doubt be lifelong, but I have never been more thankful for any work in my life. I know no other way to say it: God finally got me to a place where I made myself sick. Oh, I still get plenty of glances at my self-centeredness, but never without a good wave of nausea. God and I now have a term for it in our prayer time. Don't expect something deeply intellectual or theological. We just call it my "self-stuff." Almost every day I ask God to help me address any active "self-stuff" and nail it to the cross. I literally name anything He brings to mind and look it straight in the face, even if it makes me cry. The following terms fall under the category of "self-stuff." Give them a good look:

- self-exaltation, self-protection,
- self-righteousness, self-will,
- self-loathing, self-worship,
- self-serving, self-promotion,
- self-indulgence, self-absorption,
- self-delusion, self-pity, self-sufficiency.

Did I leave anything out? Is that some stuff, or what? If you think of others, by all means, add them to my list. Self, self, self! May it be enough to make a "self" sick! Here's the big lie: Satan has convinced us that putting down our self-stuff is some huge sacrifice. Oh, beloved, what deception! Our self-stuff is what makes us most miserable! What an albatross our self-absorption is.

I cannot stress strongly enough that getting over the self-stuff is a daily challenge. As long as we inhabit this tent of flesh, it will rise up in us. We must choose to "deny [ourselves] and take up [our] cross daily" (Luke 9:23). The challenge demands total honesty before God. Remember, He never convicts us to condemn us. He wants to liberate us. Oh, God, so deal with self in each of us that when You read our thoughts, You will find stronger and stronger evidences of Your own.

Define a biblical view of greatness. How should it look on you? What must it be sure not to consist of? _____

_____

_____

_____

_____

_____

_____

Praying God's Word Today

Lord, You have told us in Your Word to clothe ourselves with humility toward one another, because You resist the proud but give grace to the humble. Help me then, I pray, to humble myself under Your mighty hand, so that You may exalt me in due time (1 Pet. 5:5–6).

DAY 51

Blasted Unbelievers

Before You Begin
Read Luke 9:51–56

Stop and Consider

When the disciples James and John saw this, they said, "Lord, do You want us to call down fire from heaven to consume them?" (v. 54).

Try to describe spiritual pride in its most awful terms. What does it look like in others? What does it look like in you? _____

_____

_____

Gauge your heart right now for the lost and unbelieving. What would it take to quicken in you an urgency for sharing Christ and grieving over others' souls? _____

_____

_____

_____

James and John remind me of two little boys holding their popguns, jumping up and down, pleading: "Let me shoot! Let me! Let me!" The difference is, this was no game. They wanted to call down the fire of God. They were eagerly asking for permission to be agents of massive, irreversible destruction.

Nothing is more permanent or terrifying than the destruction of the lost. We ought to be scared to death to wish such a thing on anyone. Eternity is a long time. So even when punishment comes to the terribly wicked, we are wise to remember with deep sobriety, humility, and thankfulness that only grace saves us from a like sentence.

We know this world is filled with wickedness. As Christ's present-day disciples, we will no doubt be offended when people reject the Savior the way the Samaritan village did on this day. God's desire, however, is for us to pray for His mercy, for His Holy Spirit's conviction, and for their repentance rather than their judgment. Christ said even of those who hammered the nails into His flesh, "Father, forgive them, for they do not know what they are doing" (Luke 23:34).

God is indeed the righteous Judge. When Christ returns, those who rejected Him will literally cry to the mountains, "'Fall on us!' and to the hills, 'Cover us!'" (Luke 23:30). Judgment is coming, but may the thought of it cause us to weep, plead, and pray. Never boast about being saved while others are not. Only one thing stands between us and the lost: a blood-stained cross.

Dear one, I know this may be coming across to you as quite harsh. But please know that this message was written with such love. I have been the worst of transgressors in so many ways. No matter how common these attitudes are, they are terribly offensive to Christ. May we humble ourselves before Him, repent, and daily choose to lay down the albatross of our own egos.

Oh, God, give us a longing—not for the sin of this world to be judged—but for the sinners of this world to be forgiven.

Praying God's Word Today

O Lord, help me have a righteous fear of You as I read Your Word that says, "Do not judge, so that you won't be judged" (Matt. 7:1). Instead, may I (as Paul did) feel the pains of childbirth for others until Christ is formed in them (Gal. 4:19). May I walk in wisdom toward outsiders, making the most of the time. May my speech always be gracious, seasoned with salt, so that I may know how to answer each person (Col. 4:5–6). _____

_____

_____

_____

_____

_____

_____

_____

_____

_____

_____

DAY 52

Hey, It's Not Me

Before You Begin
Read Luke 10:1–16

Stop and Consider

Whoever listens to you listens to Me. Whoever rejects you rejects Me.
And whoever rejects Me rejects the One who sent Me (v. 16).

In what ways do you experience rejection or disapproval because of your relationship with Jesus Christ? _____

_____

_____

What are some of the hardest parts of this to deal with? Why is being misunderstood such a normal place for Christians to be? _____

_____

_____

_____

This concept Jesus taught in verse 16 is something else I love so much about Him. In many ways, He says to those who belong to Him and who seek to do His will: "Don't take rejection personally. Let me take it for you."

We see this principle at work in Acts 9. Saul set out to persecute Christians, but Jesus came along and knocked him off his donkey. "Falling to the ground, [Saul] heard a voice saying to him, 'Saul, Saul, why do you persecute me?'" (Acts 9:4). Beloved, can you accept that Christ takes very personally the unfair things that happen to you? Consider a couple of reasons why we are wise to let Christ assume our rejections:

1) Only Christ can take rejection without being personally incapacitated or hindered by it. Who can begin to estimate the mileage Satan gets from rejection? We have an overwhelming tendency to take it personally. From a bit of rejection Satan can get anything from a mile of discouragement to a thousand miles of despair. But Christ says to us, "Let Me take it personally for you. It can *hurt* Me, but it can't hinder Me." David had it right when he wrote, "Contend, O Lord, with those who contend with me; fight against those who fight against me. Take up shield and buckler; arise and come to my aid" (Ps. 35:1–2).

2) Only Christ can properly respond to rejection. We are often powerless to do anything about it. In fact, our attempts at responding to it often make the situation worse. We don't fully understand what lies at the heart of rejection. We cannot judge another person's intention or motive. But Romans 2:2 assures us that "God's judgment against those who do such things is based on truth."

I love to hear Keith say, "Elizabeth, let me worry about that." In essence, Christ says the same thing to us. If we suffer rejection, let Him worry about it. Let Him take it personally so we don't have to. Besides, even Jesus has Someone to shield Him from the blow of rejection. Take one last look at Luke 10:16. "He who listens to you listens to me; he who rejects you rejects me, *but he who rejects me rejects him who sent me.*" Trust His big shoulders, beloved, to be strong enough to take whatever others dish out.

Praying God's Word Today

Lord Jesus, as uncomfortable as it can sometimes be, I must take You at Your Word: I am blessed when people insult me and persecute me and falsely say every kind of evil against me because of You (Matt. 5:11). The person who rejects Your truth does not reject man, but You, Lord, who have given us Your Holy Spirit (1 Thess. 4:8). May I live with this understanding, even when it hurts.

DAY 53

Watch Me Dance

Before You Begin

Read Luke 10:17–24

Stop and Consider

In that same hour He rejoiced in the Holy Spirit and said,

"I praise You, Father, Lord of heaven and earth" (v. 21).

How much fun is it to see Jesus enthusiastically worshiping with His disciples? How does that square with your view of Him and His public demeanor? _____

_____

_____

How much a part of your life is worship and spiritual celebration? _____

_____

_____

_____

Jesus sent out seventy-two disciples to teach and heal, instructing them to "ask the Lord of the harvest . . . to send out workers" into His harvest field (Luke 10:2). He sent these disciples out "two by two." The original language phrase for this is *ana duo*.

I love the fact that Christ sanctions companionship in the work of the gospel! The point is not the magic number of "two" (as opposed to three or four). The point is simply togetherness. Exceptions to this exist, of course, when we are called to stand alone, but the standard rule of our lives in Christ is far more often the fellowship, protection, accountability, and double dividends of joint service.

I can hardly describe the joy my coworkers in the gospel bring me. My best friend and I met each other by serving together in Mothers' Day Out over twenty years ago. God called us to work *ana duo,* and we've been a duo ever since! Few things can add to our lives like the fellowship of serving together. I didn't want you to miss that point in this passage.

But today, I want to look more carefully at what happened when the seventy-two returned, rejoicing with something that resembled amazement. In verse 17 they essentially said, "Wow! It happened just like You said it would, Jesus! Even the demons were subject to us in Your name! What a rush!"

Sandwiched between expressions of jubilation, Christ took a quick moment to remind them that they had a greater motivation for rejoicing than this: *their names were written in heaven.* So although we see Him celebrate their victories, we also see Him teaching them to base their joy on something far more reliable than accomplishments and abilities. He wanted them—and he wants us—to understand that the greatest cause we have for joy is not what we do but who we are. We are children of the eternal *El Elyon.* Our names are recorded in heaven. We are very wise to find our joy in who we are because of Him, rather than what we can do because of Him.

But now let's enjoy these two awesome moments of celebration. Verse 21 tells us Jesus was "full of joy through the Holy Spirit." Here's a place where the original language is so much fun. In verse 17, the word for the joy of the disciples is *chara,* meaning essentially

what you'd assume: "rejoicing" and "gladness." The word switches in verse 21, however, to a far more intense original word. The word for Jesus' joy is *agalliao*, meaning "to exult, leap for joy, to show one's joy by leaping and skipping, denoting excessive or ecstatic joy and delight." In the Septuagint of the Psalms, this idea often spoke of "rejoicing with song and dance."

Someone may ask, "Do you expect me to believe Christ jumped up and down with ecstatic joy?" I don't have one bit of trouble believing it!

"Could the word simply mean He rejoiced in His heart?" Possibly, but the essence of the word *agalliao* is what happens when the word *chara* gets physical! You may apply it either way, but I prefer to jump up and down with Jesus. With all my heart, I believe Christ Jesus was and is demonstrative.

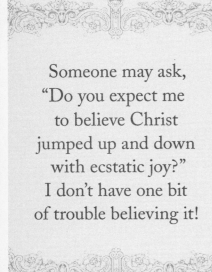

Someone may ask, "Do you expect me to believe Christ jumped up and down with ecstatic joy?" I don't have one bit of trouble believing it!

But what would cause Jesus to leap with ecstatic joy in this scene (whether physically or internally)? At least two catalysts for colossal joy appear in these verses:

1) Satan's defeat. "I saw Satan fall like lightning from heaven" (v. 18). According to Revelation 12:10–12, Satan was cast out of heaven for pride, rebellion, and his desire to usurp the Most High (see also Ezek. 28:16–17; Isa. 14:12–13). At the risk of oversimplification, Satan has attempted to get back at God ever since by targeting those He loves.

But we who are in Christ possess the power through God's Word and His Spirit to avoid being defeated by the evil one. Problem is, we don't always exercise that power. The disciples in Luke 10 did. They exercised the authority He had given them, and Christ was ecstatic! At the end of the contest, the scoreboard read: Believers 72, Satan 0. That was a score Jesus could have spilled His popcorn over! When was the last time you got excited over the defeat of the devil? Notice, too, the other side of the equation:

2) The servants' victory. "I praise you, Father, Lord of heaven and earth, because you have hidden these things from the wise and learned and have revealed them to little children" (v. 21). You see, the wise and learned of this world are often too sophisticated to throw caution to the wind and believe they're capable of doing something they've never thought possible. If we stay in our neat little perimeters of safe sophistication where we walk by sight and not by faith, we'll never have room to leap and skip with Jesus in ecstatic joy.

Oh, beloved, give Him a chance to leap and dance over you! Dare to do what He's calling you to do! And don't always be so reasonable. I have a feeling there's one thing Christ likes better than leaping and skipping and dancing over you. How about *with* you? When you hear that victory music playing, get up out of that chair and shake a leg.

We all have things that get us excited. But are they the same things that get Jesus excited? What kind of kingdom celebrations should really jazz our spirits? _____

_____

_____

_____

_____

_____

_____

PRAYING GOD'S WORD TODAY

Lord, this Scripture passage helps me see so much of You in David, the "man after Your own heart," who danced before You with all His might (2 Sam. 6:14). My heart echoes his words today in celebrating "how happy is the one whose transgression is forgiven, whose sin is covered! . . . Be glad in the Lord and rejoice, you righteous ones; shout for joy, all you upright in heart" (Ps. 32:1, 11). Hallelujah! _____

_____

_____

_____

_____

_____

_____

_____

_____

_____

_____

_____

_____

DAY 54

Do You Really
Want to Know?

Before You Begin
Read Luke 10:25–37

Stop and Consider

Just then an expert in the law stood up to test Him, saying,
"Teacher, what must I do to inherit eternal life?" (v. 25).

What are some of the religious questions you hear people asking today? What is most often misunderstand about the ways of Christ and the reality of faith in Him? _____

_____

_____

_____

What would you say to someone who believes a good life is the true roadmap to heaven?

_____

_____

_____

Scripture describes Jesus' questioner as an expert in the law. His job was to interpret the law of Moses the way modern lawyers interpret the constitution. He considered himself such an expert that he intended to make Jesus look foolish. The problem is, you can't find a subject on which Christ isn't the ultimate expert. The expert in the law didn't know that Christ knew the drill far better than he did.

So Jesus responded to him with a question that means little to us but was very familiar to the lawyer. He asked, "How do you read it?" This question was used constantly among scribes and lawyers. One would ask the other his interpretation on a certain matter. Before he would give his answer, he would say, "How do you read it?" This way, the one who asked the question ended up having to "go first."

(Of course, you and I know what the scribe didn't know. Christ not only wrote the law, He came to fulfill it. The resident expert in the law was way over his head when he threw a pop quiz at the author of the Book.)

Being forced to "go first," the legal mind delivered the correct answer according to Old Testament law: "'Love the Lord your God with all your heart and with all your soul and with all your strength and with all your mind'; and 'Love your neighbor as yourself'" (Luke 10:27). The conversation could have stopped when Jesus said, "Do this and you will live" (v. 28). Instead, the lawyer had to ask one more question: "And who is my neighbor?" (v. 29).

Do you hear a change in tone? The man wanted to justify himself—to show himself righteous—but why? Who said he wasn't? Christ didn't say a single condemning word to him. Jesus simply told him his answer was correct and to go live his answer.

But the man couldn't let the matter go. In Christ's presence, the lawyer felt condemned by his own words. He knew God intended for His people to help those in need. So the lawyer attempted to justify himself by splitting hairs with his definition of a neighbor. His immediate defense mechanism was to try to start an argument. Not an unfamiliar tactic, is it? We've all been experts at that one!

Jesus answered the man's question with one of the most repeated stories in the New Testament, telling of a priest and a Levite on their way home to Jericho from Jerusalem who both ignored a man that had been beaten and robbed along the road. But the irony in their unwillingness to help would have been more obvious to the lawyer than to us. He would have quickly understood that they were on their way home from the most important life work they would ever do—performing their brief tenure of service in the temple. We would expect that at no time would they have been more humbled, grateful, or willing to meet someone's needs. But that's not what happened. In fact, both the priest and the Levite passed by on the other side.

> God demands compassionate action on our part no matter how we try to hide ourselves in loopholes of terminology.

The words of the law in Exodus 23 make the actions of the priest and Levite even more incriminating. Moses wrote, "If you come across your enemy's ox or donkey wandering off, be sure to take it back to him. If you see the donkey of someone who hates you fallen down under its load, do not leave it there; be sure you help him with it" (vv. 4–5).

Don't you praise God, though, for the third passerby in the scene? Our common name for this parable would have been an oxymoron to many Jews of that era. Most would have believed there was no such thing as a "good" Samaritan. They were considered little more than mongrels. Half-breed dogs. That's precisely why Christ interjected the Samaritan into the play.

Scripture tells us the Samaritan saw the man and took pity on him. You would think that at least the priest and the Levite would have done the right thing because of their positions, even if they *felt* the wrong thing. In sharp contrast, the Samaritan came upon the scene with no obligation whatsoever, and everything within him was deeply moved with compassion. He didn't just do what was right. He felt it.

Sometimes good at its best is when the law of the heart eclipses the law of the land. Stepping across a boundary to help is sometimes our first introduction to the commonality of humanity on the other side. Offering help in a time of need can be the first step to overcoming God-dishonoring prejudice.

Don't forget the reason Jesus told the story. Whom did He say was our neighbor? I am reminded of an Old Testament verse that describes a neighbor at Passover. Because all of the lamb was required to be consumed at the Passover observance, Exodus 12 explains that a family was to share with their nearest neighbor if their household was too small for a whole lamb.

From Jesus' parable we can see that our neighbor is the person with a need—the broken one. In terms of Exodus 12, our neighbor is one with whom we can share the Lamb. As people who have been passed over by the angel of death, we are called to share the Lamb.

What justifications have you used to avoid caring for a particular person or class of people that you don't really like to be around? _____

_____

_____

_____

_____

_____

_____

PRAYING GOD'S WORD TODAY

Father, I hear again Your admonition that says, "When it is in your power, don't withhold good from the one to whom it is due. Don't say to your neighbor, 'Go away! Come back later. I'll give it tomorrow'—when it is there with you" (Prov. 3:27–28). May I not owe anyone anything except my love, for as You have said, "The one who loves another has fulfilled the law" (Rom. 13:8). This is the kind of person I want You to create in me.

DAY 55

Good and Best

BEFORE YOU BEGIN
Read Luke 10:38–42

STOP AND CONSIDER

The Lord answered her, "Martha, Martha, you are worried and upset about many things, but one thing is necessary. Mary has made the right choice, and it will not be taken away from her" (vv. 41–42).

Are you the type of person who's often "worried and upset"? What preoccupations and obligations keep you feeling that way? _____

_____

_____

What would become of Marys if not for Marthas? And to Marthas if not for Marys?

_____

_____

_____

This passage is not a contrast between good and bad. It's a contrast between good and better. Martha was a good woman. Jesus loved her very much, apron and all, as confirmed in John 11:5—"Jesus loved Martha and her sister and Lazarus." Her joy and satisfaction, however, were sacrificed on the altar of self-appointed service. Recognizing Martha's positives and negatives, let's explore some applications together.

1) Martha opened her home, but Mary opened her heart (vv. 38–39). Don't miss the fact that Martha opened her home to Jesus. Not Lazarus, the head of the house. Nor Mary, the depth of the house. It was the "hands" of the house that invited Jesus in. Otherwise, Mary wouldn't have had a set of feet at which to sit, nor would Lazarus have had a friend with which to recline. Martha's hospitality brought Him there. If only Martha had understood that Christ wanted her heart more than He wanted her home.

2) Distraction is the noble person's biggest hindrance to listening (vv. 39–40). Martha wasn't stopping her ears and refusing to listen. She was simply "distracted." In this way, we've all been Marthas! How many times have we reached the car after a church service only to realize that we missed half the message due to a distraction?

Now imagine that the church service was meeting in your den while you were preparing lunch! Talk about distracting? The Greek word for "distracted" in verse 40 is *perispao*, meaning "to draw different ways at the same time, hence to distract with cares and responsibilities." Can we relate? You see, our culture may be entirely different, but women have had the same challenges since the beginning of time.

3) Sometimes ministry can be the biggest distraction to the pursuit of true intimacy with God (v. 40). I've heard the saying many times, "If Satan can't make us bad, he'll make us busy." Actually, he can't make us anything, but he gets a lot of cooperation. I am reminded of our study on the good Samaritan. How wise of our God to place these two accounts back-to-back in Scripture. First we saw an incriminating look at servants of God who ministered in the temple but refused to help a dying man. Now we catch a look at a servant who was so busy helping, she couldn't hear from the heart of God.

4) Martha forgot to keep the "pre" in preparation (v. 40). Understand that the preparations she made were not frivolous. They were important! By doing them, Martha served Christ appropriately and enhanced the atmosphere in which He taught. Very likely she served a meal and made sure all the arrangements were made for His comfort and the exercise of His own ministry. These preparations were important. They just weren't limited to the "pre." The issue is that she continued all her duties when the time came to sit at Christ's feet and listen.

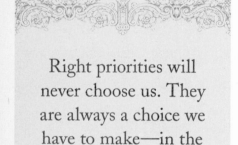

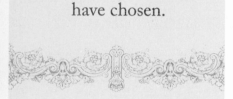

Right priorities will never choose us. They are always a choice we have to make—in the midst of many other good ones we could have chosen.

I speak at many conferences during which the event's leadership either never makes it into the sanctuary or, when they do, they never lose that harried and distracted look. Recently, however, I spoke at a conference where the leadership was truly the most participatory, involved group during the Bible study. When I inquired later, they said, "Oh, we worked really hard in advance to get everything finished so we could relax when the time came." They made all the preparations, but when the time came, the men of the church and several hired caterers served while they attended. What wisdom we find in keeping the "pre" in preparation!

5) Those distracted by service are often those who miss how much Jesus cares (v. 40). I have a feeling if someone had asked Mary at the end of the day if Christ cared about her, she would have answered affirmatively without hesitation. But Martha came to Christ and asked, "Don't You care?"

Beloved, Christ's love for us never changes. However, our sense of His loving care can change dramatically from time to time. And I believe the determining factor in whether we sense His love or not is our willingness to abide in Him, to seek to practice a relationship in which we develop a keener awareness of His presence.

Sometimes we are so shocked when a seasoned servant of God confesses that he or she is struggling with belief and awareness of God's loving care. We might think, "You of all people! You are such a wonderful servant of God. How can you doubt for a moment how much He cares for you?" Could it be that somehow service has distracted them from abundant, life-giving intimacy? Don't neglect to give Him ample opportunities to lavish you with the love He always feels for you.

6) Many things are important, but only one thing is necessary (v. 42). In our fight for right priorities, many things vie for the top of the heap, but only one is necessary. Ultimately, our relationship with Christ is the one thing we cannot do without. Christ's message is not that we should neglect family and other responsibilities to pray and to study the Bible. His message is that many things are important, but one thing is essential: Him. Incidentally, Mary turned out to be one of the greatest servants of all, lavishing Christ with her most expensive offerings (see John 12). She learned. So can we.

What are the main choices standing between you and a more consistent experience of living by God's best priorities, not merely settling for good ones? _____

_____

_____

_____

_____

_____

PRAYING GOD'S WORD TODAY

Lord, You remind us in Your Word that the end of all things is near. Therefore, You exhort us to be clear-headed and disciplined for prayer, and above all to keep our love for one another at full strength, since love covers a multitude of sins. And yes, You even tell us to be hospitable towards others, but without complaining (1 Pet. 4:7–9). So I pray for Your help in filling me with these godly attributes, in order that I may honor You with both my heart and actions, in order that I may know and express Your love in greater ways.

DAY 56

*No More
Mr. Strong Man*

JESUS

Before You Begin

Read Luke 11:14–23

Stop and Consider

When a strong man, fully armed, guard his estate, his possessions are secure.
But when one stronger than he attacks and overpowers him, he takes from
him all his weapons he trusted in, and divides up his plunder (vv. 21–22).

What has Satan stolen from you? What have you lost along the way that you know the Lord
will one day reclaim for you? _____

_____

_____

What are some of the "weapons" Satan has trusted in as he's battled against you? How
could you use this knowledge to shield yourself from his attacks? _____

_____

_____

_____

Just as God is possessive over His holy house, you can be sure Satan is possessive over his unholy house. Therefore, we can't help but deal with the reality of Luke 11:21, assuming that he is the "strong man" in Jesus' parable. But thank God we have verse 22 to follow it up, where we learn some valuable things about our Jesus, our One and Only:

1) *Satan may be strong, but Christ is "stronger."* We are wise neither to overestimate nor underestimate Satan's power. But even though we are no match for him, he is no match for God. We may be at war with a very powerful enemy, but we who are in Christ are at peace with a far more powerful God. As Paul taught, we can now take our stand against the enemy because we are "strong in the Lord and in his mighty power" (Eph. 6:10).

2) *Christ will attack and overcome Satan.* Satan is a defeated foe. The defeating blows actually came through a hammer on the nails of the cross. Christ finished the work when He willingly gave His life for our sins. So God is now biding His time until His kingdom calendar has been accomplished and all who will receive His salvation are redeemed. Then one day, God's finger is going to point right at the strong man, and Satan is going to wish he'd never existed.

3) *Our someone stronger is going to take away Satan's armor and divide up the spoils.* Do you know what this means to us? Jesus Christ is going to take back what Satan has stolen from us! And not all the spoils have to wait until we're in heaven!

I can readily cite a personal example. Even though Satan stole many things from me through my childhood victimization, I am finally ready to say that God has given me back more than my enemy took. The enemy has fought against me with his weapons of shame, secrecy, and deception, but the plunder my Lord has won back for me has finally tipped the scale. Through the many response letters I've received from my book *Breaking Free: Making Liberty in Christ a Reality in Life*, I believe I can now say that the grace gift of seeing others helped through the power of the Holy Spirit has begun to outweigh the many years of pain that resulted from the abuse. The strong man may have put up a good fight, but his fight was no match for my stronger Man's muscle.

PRAYING GOD'S WORD TODAY

O Lord, because of You, even the captives of the mighty man will be taken, and the prey of the tyrant will be delivered. For You will contend with the one who contends with us, and You will save Your children from his grasp. Then all flesh will know that You are the Lord, our Savior and Redeemer, the Mighty One of Jacob" (Isa. 49:25–26). How I praise You for such limitless power and faithful, covenant love. _____

_____

_____

_____

_____

_____

_____

_____

_____

_____

_____

_____

DAY 57

Filled,
Not Just Fixed

Before You Begin
Read Luke 11:24–28

Stop and Consider
When an unclean spirit comes out of a man, it roams through
waterless places looking for rest, and not finding rest, it then says:
"I'll go back to my house where I came from" (v. 24).

What has the Lord delivered you from in the past? What sins and strongholds have you
actually experienced His victory over? _____

_____

_____

Has Satan been trying anything lately to lure you back in? Have you experienced times of
significant relapse? What have those periods been like? _____

_____

_____

_____

Satan is a lot of things, but creative is not often one of them. He ordinarily sticks to what has worked in the past. I've experienced this personally when he has attempted to return to an area in my life where he held a previous stronghold—even though he's already been forced to leave.

Beloved, listen carefully. We were created by God to be inhabited by His Spirit. We were not created to be empty. The vacuum in every human life does not yearn to be fixed. It yearns to be filled. God can deliver us from a terribly oppressive stronghold, but if we don't fill the void with Him, we are terribly susceptible to a relapse.

My Sunday school class has what we call VIPs—Victors in Process. Every quarter, members who need extra prayer and accountability come before our class for special notice. Throughout the quarter, they can hardly get through the door without lots of hugs and direct questions about how they're doing. One of our recent VIPs was a beautiful young woman recovering from a fierce cocaine addiction. How wise she was to realize that she couldn't just "get clean." If she was going to be safe, she had to fill the cavernous void left behind by cocaine with the satisfying, liberating filling of the Holy Spirit.

I'm telling you, a second round of the same demonic stronghold can be more powerful than the first. What a frightening prospect for someone who isn't sealed by the Holy Spirit (see Eph. 1:13; 4:30). Sure, most of us are at higher risk of *oppression* than *possession*, but the principle still applies: once we've been delivered from a stronghold, if we make ourselves vulnerable to it again, our second encounter may be far worse.

This is because Satan hates to lose. If he was defeated once, given the opportunity, he'll try harder the next time. Furthermore, a second onslaught can cause such discouragement and feelings of hopelessness within the victim, she feels weaker than ever. Satan also knows that the empty space—if left uninhabited by Christ—leaves the victim with a voracious appetite. So let's repeat this concept until it's engraved in our cranium: victory is not determined as much by what we've been delivered *from* as by what we've been delivered *to*. It's not enough to be swept clean and put in order. We must be filled full of God.

Praying God's Word Today

I pray, Lord, that You would grant us, according to the riches of Your glory, to be strengthened with power through Your Spirit in our inner man, and that Christ would dwell in our hearts through faith. Being rooted and firmly established in love, may we be able to comprehend with all the saints what is the length and width, height and depth of Your love—even though it surpasses knowledge—that we may be filled with all the fullness of God (Eph. 3:16–19).

DAY 58

His Treasure,
Your Treasure

Before You Begin

Read Luke 12:1–34

Stop and Consider

The Gentile world eagerly seeks all these things, and your
Father knows that you need them. But seek His kingdom,
and these things will be provided for you" (vv. 30–31).

In what ways is your life unlike that of the ordinary unbeliever? In what ways, though, is
it almost indistinguishable, nearly impossible to tell you apart? _____

_____

_____

What's the difference between what an unbeliever feels about herself and what you feel
about yourself as a redeemed child of God? _____

_____

_____

If we truly believe what God says about our value to Him, our lives will be dramatically altered. Based on this long segment of Scripture from Luke 12, which includes a wide mix of teachings and parables and different kinds of audiences, I want to suggest five ways such a belief makes a difference.

1) Believing our great value to God frees us from much hypocrisy. Christ opened His bold declarations in Luke 12 with a warning against hypocrisy. The primary meaning of the word is "pretending." Please give special attention to His specific audience. Although He was surrounded by crowds of unbelievers and religious leaders, Jesus began to speak "first to his disciples" (Luke 12:1). True disciples who follow Christ and lead others to do likewise face great temptation to be hypocritical. Christ warned, "Be on your guard" (v. 1). In other words, if we're going to live free of hypocrisy, we must proactively guard against it. The bottom line of hypocrisy is the need for people to think more highly of us than we really are. Let's face it. It's easier to act than to clean up our act.

Hypocrisy has so much to prove. Ironically, it seeks to prove that which is not even true. But when we accept our real value to God, we don't have anything left to prove. We can be real because we are of great value to the only True Judge.

2) Believing our great value to God frees us from unnecessary fear. Luke 12:4 comes like a shock wave to our systems: "I tell you, my friends, do not be afraid of those who kill the body and after that can do no more." Why do we have such difficulty grasping Jesus' point of view? Because we are far more convinced of the "here and now" than the "after that." Eternity is a far greater reality than this short breath of time. If we are in His fold and are called His friends, Christ's word to us is, "Don't be afraid; you are worth more."

Keith and I keep a bird feeder on the back porch. I watch the sparrows scatter the seed and flutter their wings. They are not beautiful like other birds that grace our yard. They are plain and ordinary. But I love knowing that God never forgets a single one of them. When fear seeks to assail me, I go to the window and am reminded again—if He cares for them, He most assuredly cherishes me. After this short breath is a long "after that."

3) Believing our great value to God frees us to acknowledge Him shamelessly. Verse 8 assures us that Christ Jesus can hardly wait to acknowledge us before the very "angels of God"—even after all our frailties and failures! (Check out Jude 24.) If He is unashamed of us in all our imperfections, how can we be ashamed of Him, our Redeemer and our Deliverer?

Yet at one time or another, all of us have faced the temptation to shrink away from openly acknowledging Christ. I've learned one of the best ways to get over these attacks of shame. Do it over and over until it loses its intimidation! Just be honest with Him and *tell* Him you're afraid. Tell Him all the reasons why. Then ask for the power of the Holy Spirit to come upon you and make you a powerful witness (see Acts 1:8). He will! Then one day, He'll acknowledge you before the angels!

> One of the best ways to become more acquainted with the heart of God is to search the Scriptures and study the things He values most.

4) Believing our great value to God frees us from the need for riches. In verse 15, Christ warns us to also "be on [our] guard" against all kinds of greed. Then He reminds us of a powerful truth: "a man's life does not consist in the abundance of his possessions." Aren't you thankful for that? I'm reminded of a friend's statement: "We act out what we believe, not what we know." If we believe our value to God and believe our life does not consist in the abundance of our possessions, why then do we have such an abundance of possessions? Perhaps we know Luke 12:15 with our heads, but we really don't believe it with our hearts.

James 1:17 tells us our Father is the giver of all good gifts. Throughout all of eternity, we will be lavished in the limitless wealth of the CEO of the universe. Until then, we show ourselves to be sons and daughters of the one true God when we give, give, and give. Let's keep shoving that abundance out the door to help others in need, and God will lay up treasures for us in His own divine storage lot.

5) Believing our great value to God frees us from much worry. "Life is more than food" (v. 23). I need a needlepoint of that for my kitchen! How about you? The issue of food, however, is not the point. The point is *worry*. I'm not sure many things compare to the challenge of ceasing to worry. Maybe one reason why is because we have so many prime opportunities to practice it! But you know what? We're never going to overcome worry by eliminating reasons to worry. Rest assured, life isn't going to suddenly fix itself. God wills that we overcome worry even when overwhelmed by reasons to worry.

Christ summed up the futility of worry in verses 25 and 26. We can't add a minute to our life by worrying. Simply put, worry is useless—even when we're worrying about the lives of our children. I am prone to worry somewhat about myself but endlessly over them. Yet all our worry, even when done in the name of love, can accomplish absolutely nothing. When will we learn to turn our worry effort into prayer?

The prescription for worry is trust—taking God at His Word. Make a list of all your reasons to worry, then write the word TRUST in big, bold letters on top of your list.

_____

_____

_____

_____

_____

_____

Praying God's Word Today

Father, I'm reminded that You said to the children of Israel, "You are a holy people belonging to the LORD your God. The LORD your God has chosen you to be His own possession out of all the peoples on the face of the earth" (Deut. 7:6). I know this applies to Your children today, as well. I will never understand Your reasons for loving us this way, but I rest in it at this moment. May it not only comfort me but also change me, making me secure enough to serve You with abandon.

DAY 59

Leave the Light On

Before You Begin
Read Luke 12:35–40

Stop and Consider

You must be like people waiting for their master to return from the wedding banquet so that when he comes and knocks, they can open the door for him at once (v. 36).

What keeps you most distracted from awaiting Christ's return? _____

_____

_____

What are some very practical things you could be doing to constantly remind yourself to be scanning the skies, looking forward to His appearing? _____

_____

_____

_____

_____

Jesus told the disciples a set of interlaced parables in Luke 12 about being ready for His return. We'll look at the first one today. The point of each dealt with watchfulness and doing what Christ assigns us to do. Christ wants His people to be ready and waiting. No matter whether you're a pretribulationalist, a post-tribulationalist, an amillennialist, a dispensationalist, or have no clue what any of these terms even mean, Christ is coming back. Every eye will see Him.

Some things about God's ways make me grin . . . like the way He knows our tendency to play amateur prophet. He puts all of us in our date-setting places by basically saying, "The only thing I'll tell you about My next visit is that you won't be expecting Me." The urgency is to be ready at all times. "Keep your lamps burning" (Luke 12:35).

Our version of keeping our lamps burning is leaving a light on at night for someone out late. One of the shocks of the empty nest is no longer having someone to "wait up for." Those of us who have older children have experienced the late-night difficulty of falling into a deep sleep before they get home. We can doze perhaps, but we don't fully sleep until they're safe inside. Even though waiting up is exhausting, it's a reminder of close family relationships and responsibility. At this particular season in my life, my heart is encouraged to know that we still have Someone for whom to "leave the light on."

Several years ago a precious friend of mine lost her only son, a young adult. Five years later she lost her husband. I have ached for her aloneness. But I am so grateful that those of us in Christ always have Someone for whom we can wait expectantly at all times. Christ calls on us to be watching for Him when He returns—not inactively, mind you, but as servants (v. 37). Luke 12:38 tells us, "It will be good for those servants whose master finds them ready, even if he comes in the second or third watch of the night."

Christ's desire is that we live in such close involvement with Him that all we lack is seeing Him face-to-face. Oh, that God would create in each of us such an acute awareness and belief of His presence that we won't be caught off guard! That our faith will simply be made sight! That we'll be gloriously shocked but unashamed!

PRAYING GOD'S WORD TODAY

O Lord, may I never be like those who doubt or scoff at Your Word, who are tempted to say, "Where is the promise of His coming? For ever since the fathers fell asleep, all things continue as they have since the beginning of creation" (2 Pet. 3:4). I know that with You, Lord, one day is like 1,000 years, and 1,000 years like one day (2 Pet. 3:8). Create in me, therefore, an expectant longing for Your appearing. May my lamps be ever burning.

DAY 60

Service
While You Wait

Before You Begin
Read Luke 12:41–48

Stop and Consider

That slave who knew his master's will and didn't prepare
himself or do it will be severely beaten (v. 47).

Is it fair for God to hold spiritual leaders to a higher level of accountability than others? How
would you agree or disagree with that statement? _____

_____

_____

What have you been given by God in terms of teaching, ability, and heritage that He will
hold you accountable for using in His service? _____

_____

_____

For those with a knowledge of God, the cost of wickedness during our wait for Jesus' return is astronomical. I'm not sure we ever hear stronger words out of His mouth than these: "He will cut him to pieces and assign him a place with the unbelievers" (v. 46).

I believe Christ was most likely addressing His remarks to the people He described in Luke 11:52: "Woe to you experts in the law, because you have taken away the key to knowledge. You yourselves have not entered, and you have hindered those who were entering." I'd like to suggest that the picture of the head servant beating the menservants and maidservants while the master was away (Luke 12:45) could easily represent spiritual abuse at the hands of religious leaders. God will hold those of us who are leaders responsible for this.

I can think of many examples, but one instantly raises its ugly head in my mind—the preacher who beats and bangs hellfire and damnation on his pulpit, piously condemning his flock for all manner of evil, while abusing his wife and children at home. I wish I could tell you that I've only heard such a testimony once or twice. Let me stress that I still believe the far greater population of Christians resist that kind of hypocrisy, but spiritual abuse of this nature exists far more than we want to believe.

Another form of spiritual abuse is using Scripture or the name of God to manipulate others. I have very little doubt we will be called to account for the times we have used God's name to get what we want. Christ despises all forms of human oppression. A huge penalty awaits those who possess a knowledge of God yet persist in meanness and self-indulgence. Forgive me if my temperature on this matter is showing. If not for the authentic examples of godliness, I would despair over all the abuse I've seen in the religious community.

But I also know the future punishment of the unfaithful will be fair: "From everyone who has been given much, much will be demanded" (v. 48). That's fair. But that's serious. I have been given so much. I must accept the fact that much is also required. Here is our joy and security in the midst of much required: Christ is never the author of spiritual abuse. Every single thing required of us will be amply rewarded far beyond our imagination.

PRAYING GOD'S WORD TODAY

Lord, remind me afresh today that it is already the hour for us to wake up from our sleep, for our salvation is nearer than when we first believed. The night is nearly over, and the daylight is near. So inspire us to discard the deeds of darkness and put on the armor of light. Help us to walk in decency, as in the daylight, not in all kinds of sinful behavior. Lead us to put on the Lord Jesus Christ and make no plans to satisfy our fleshly desires (Rom. 13:11–14).

DAY 61

Sure Thing

BEFORE YOU BEGIN
Read Luke 13:31–33

STOP AND CONSIDER

He said to them, "Go tell that fox, 'Look! I'm driving out demons and performing
healings today and tomorrow, and on the third day I will complete My work" (v. 32).

Was Jesus being rude? Are there times in life when directness like this is not just allowed
but is actually what the Lord would like to see from you? _____

_____

_____

What "Herods" are after you today, seeking to kill what God has started in you? _____

_____

_____

_____

I love Christ's last five words in verse 32: "I will complete My work."

• Not "I will complete My work if all the conditions are right."

• Not "I will complete My work if you cooperate with me."

• Not "I will complete My work if I'm still alive."

"I will complete My work." It's that simple. The New International Version renders His statement, "I will reach My goal." No ifs, ands, or buts.

"I will." Period.

Beloved, find security in the fact that nothing is haphazard about the activity of God. He has a goal, and He has a definitive plan that is to be executed precisely according to His will.

You no doubt noticed Christ's symbolic phraseology in this verse, as well. In a sense, Christ spoke in the style of a parable. When He spoke of the miracle activity He would be doing "today and tomorrow," followed by "the third day," He spoke not in the immediate sense but in a future tense. Because of our hindsight advantage, we hear the unmistakable hint of the three days beginning with the cross and ending with His resurrection. In essence, Christ said, "I have a goal. I have work to do *today* toward that goal. I have work to do *tomorrow* toward that goal. But very soon that goal will be accomplished."

Perhaps Christ's use of the words "today," "tomorrow," and "the third day" suggest three segments of time in *our lives* as well. Today is our now. The third day could represent the ultimate fulfillment of God's goals for our lives. And tomorrow could represent every moment between now and then. He will complete His work in us, too.

Christ's return message to Herod emphasized that nothing could turn Him from His goal. Neither Herod nor any other power posed a threat to the plan. They would be used only as puppets to fulfill it. When we live our lives according to God's will, no Herod in the world can thwart our efforts at reaching God's goal. Not a Herod of sickness nor a Herod of crisis. Not even a Herod that seems to hand us over to death.

Praying God's Word Today

Lord God, I pray that we would be delivered from wicked and evil men, from those who do not have faith. For You are faithful, and You will strengthen and guard us from the evil one (2 Thess. 3:3). We put our full and total trust in You—the One who is faithful and who also will do it (1 Thess. 5:24).

DAY 62

Spiritual Immunity

BEFORE YOU BEGIN
Read Luke 13:34–35

STOP AND CONSIDER

Jerusalem, Jerusalem! The city who kills the prophets and stones those
who are sent to her. How often I wanted to gather your children together,
as a hen gathers her chicks under her wings, but you were not willing (v. 34).

At times when you feel the most unworthy and unacceptable by God, what surprises you
the most about His willingness to renew and restore? _____

_____

_____

Who's someone in your life who needs to know this really badly today? _____

_____

_____

_____

I want us to look today at a spiritual principle I call *immunity*—meaning, shelter from all evil imposition on God's plan. One dramatic example of this principle is found in the account of the two witnesses in Revelation 11. The elements of immunity in their experience are easy to identify:

1) The witnesses get their power from God (v. 3).

2) When they are opposed, God dramatically defends them (v. 5).

3) When they have finished their testimony, the beast kills them (v. 7).

But . . . notice that the two witnesses cannot be killed until they have finished their testimony. And even at that, their deaths are by no means a tragic end to the story. God raises them from the dead and makes a mockery of their enemy (see Rev. 11:11–12).

Although the prophecy of the two witnesses is far more dramatic than the story of our lives, they illustrate a principle God applies to us as well. When we live under the umbrella of God's authority and seek to obey His commands, the enemy may oppose us and even oppress us, but he cannot thwart the fulfillment of God's plan for us. Any permission he receives to oppose us will be issued only for the greater victory of God. Death cannot come to the obedient children of God until they have finished their testimony. When we surrender our wills to the will of the Father, we find a place of blessed immunity. Strengthened by His power and shielded by His protection, we are assured of reaching our goal.

This principle is beautifully illustrated in Luke 13:34, where we see the heart of God on display as His Son cries out for the citizens of Jerusalem to come under His sheltering wings of protection. The Old Testament paints a similar portrait in Psalm 91. These words fall around us like a down comforter from heaven. The psalmist wrote: "He who dwells in the shelter of the Most High will rest in the shadow of the Almighty" (Ps. 91:1). The implication of this verse is that a place of safety—a certain level of immunity from evil onslaughts—exists for those who choose to dwell there. The concept of *dwelling* in Psalm 91:1 is virtually synonymous with the concept of *obeying* or *remaining* in John 15:10, where Jesus tells us we abide or remain in Him and His love through our obedience.

Obedience to our Father's commands is the key to immunity from the enemy. Obedience is what positions us in the shadow of the Almighty. When we are living in obedience, any evil that comes against us will have to go through God first. Christ lived for one purpose: to do the will of the One who sent Him (see John 6:38). And because He was entirely surrendered to the will of His Father, Herod's threat in Luke 13:31 had no power over Him. When the time came, the rulers and the chief priests could be used only as puppets by God in His pursuit of greater glory.

I am convinced the same is true for us. We gain the place of immunity through obedience to His will. This explains why Christ longed to gather the children of Israel into His arms the way a hen gathers her chicks under her wings, but He did not. Why? Because they weren't willing. They chose their own will over Christ's, forfeiting the shelter of His wings. The result was desolation and defeat (see Luke 13:35; 19:43).

> When we surrender our wills to the will of the Father, we find a place of blessed immunity. We are assured of reaching our goal.

The same unwillingness can have similar results in our lives today. As believers in Christ, two different forms of immunity apply to us. All who personally receive the grace gift of God have the first kind of immunity: protection from eternal judgment. We stand in the shadow of the cross. The judgment that should have come to us came to Christ instead.

But the second kind of immunity does *not* come automatically upon our salvation. It results only when we surrender our will to the Father's will. When we bow to His authority, we become immune to defeat and all other threats to the plan of God for our personal lives. I don't mean we're immune from trouble, tribulation, or even a certain amount of oppression, but they won't be able to defeat us. Through obedience, we will possess and practice the God-given power to overcome them, and God's plan will be uninterrupted.

I know these principles are true because I've experienced them. I have complete assurance of my salvation. I am convinced that the cross has immunized me against all judgment for sin. However, I have without a doubt been temporarily defeated by the enemy and done things that were not part of God's plan for my life. By surrendering to my own will in certain seasons, I have stepped outside the shelter of the Most High. And although the enemy could not overtake me, he certainly had a field day with me.

Today, I am a living, breathing, grace-filled Plan B. But I'm a Plan B who has learned some painful lessons that have changed my practices. I presently jump out of bed with one primary plan of attack for the day: ducking under the sheltering wing of the Most High so the enemy will have to get through Him to get to me.

He yearns to lavish us with His possessive, protective love—to cover us from so many unnecessary harms. There is a secret place. Go, beloved, and hide.

Why is this different from saying that our "good works" somehow earn God's favor? Why does God only extend His promise of protection to those of His children whose wills are submitted to Him, whose hearts are obedient to Him? _____

_____

_____

_____

_____

_____

Praying God's Word Today

I call on You, God, because I know You will answer me. I pray that You—the Savior of all who seek refuge from those who rebel against Your right hand—will guard me as the apple of Your eye. Hide me in the shadow of Your wings from the wicked who treat me violently, and from the deadly enemies that surround me (Ps. 17:7–9). Lord of all, be my shelter of safety as I follow Your Word, for I put my hope in Your promise of immunity. _____

_____

_____

_____

_____

_____

_____

_____

_____

_____

_____

_____

DAY 63

When God Runs

Before You Begin
Read Luke 15:11–32

Stop and Consider
While the son was still a long way off, his father saw him
and was filled with compassion (v. 20).

In what ways have you walked out from beneath the Father's protection? _____

_____

_____

What would have happened to you if God had allowed your sinful wanderings to be cost-free? What kind of additional problems would that have caused? _____

_____

_____

_____

_____

At times I've descended from the place of appropriate repentance where I was sorry for my sins, to the place of inappropriate self-loathing where I was sorry Christ was "forced" (as if He could be) to save me. I'd find myself wishing I had been a nicer sinner. More pleasant to save.

Emotion washes over me today as I remember again: Christ came for sinners like me. He *wanted* to save me. He didn't come for the pious and perfect. Our Savior came to seek and to save the lost. The hopeless. The foolish. The weak. The depraved. In His own words: "It is not the healthy who need a doctor, but the sick. I have not come to call the righteous, but sinners to repentance" (Luke 5:31–32).

I have no idea how many times I've read and even taught the story of the prodigal son, yet it still brings me to tears. I am such a product of this kind of father love. Perhaps you are too. I've watched God take a young woman I love very much and restore her to the right road after a prodigal detour. She has cried out to me, "When will all these painful repercussions end?"

I have answered her, "Not until the very idea of straying causes you such painful flashbacks that you're hardly ever tempted to depart His will again." God wants to whisper to our hearts, "Are you sure you want to go back there again?" and hear us say, "No way do I want that kind of pain!"

Luke 15:17 tells us that the son considered the abundance of his father's hired hands and realized the insanity of starving to death. He waited to go home until his desperation exceeded his pride. That the prodigal planned what he would say hints at the difficulty of his return. I wonder if the son was pacing. And pacing. And pacing. He could see his home in the distance, but perhaps he could not bring himself to walk that last mile. He looked at his father's vast estate and glanced down at his own poor estate. His clothes were worn and filthy. Dirt under every nail. His hair long and matted or shorn to the skin to defend against lice. All at once, he became aware of his own foul smell. He was destitute. Degraded.

But the prodigal's father was looking for his son in the distance. I imagine that every day since his son's departure, his father had studied the horizon in search of his son's silhouette. Just as the starving son had longed for food, his father had yearned for him. His was a yearning so deep that no amount of work could assuage it. Family members could not replace it. No distraction could soothe it. Oh, friend, can you glimpse the heart of God? Do you realize that when you run from Him, He yearns for you every minute and cannot be distracted from His thoughts of you?

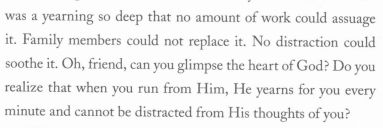

Sometimes in our rebellion we foolishly long for a searing of conscience, having no idea it would be a fate worse than death.

When God sees our poor estate and the ravaging effects of our foolish decisions, He doesn't just sit back and say, "She got what she deserved." He is filled with compassion and longs to bring us back home. Yes, we face consequences, but those consequences are a loving summons back to the Father.

In one of the most moving moments in all of Scripture, Luke 15:20 records that the father "ran" to his son. Scripture often employs anthropomorphisms—descriptions of God as if He had a human body. We sometimes read that God walked (in the midst of His people) or that He rode (on the clouds like chariots), but this is the only time in the entire Word of God when He is described as running.

What makes God run? A prodigal child turning his face toward home! How can we resist Him? How can we not reciprocate such lavish love?

When was the last time you saw an older man, the father of adult children, run? Would you picture it now? Can you feel his heart pounding in his chest? Can you hear him catching his breath? Nothing could keep him from his son.

When he reached the son, the son tried his best to give the speech he had planned, but to no avail. In all his talk of unworthiness, he didn't realize he was unworthy even before he left. He was a son not because he earned the right to be, but because he was born of his

father. He could exceed the realm of his father's shield, but he could not exceed the reach of his father's love. "Quick! Bring the best robe and put it on him. Put a ring on his finger and sandals on his feet. Bring the fattened calf and kill it. Let's have a feast and celebrate. For this son of mine was dead and is alive again; he was lost and is found" (vv. 22–24). The father literally kissed the son's past away.

Merciful Savior! Graceful God! You have kissed this prodigal's past into forgetfulness! Though mockers may accuse me, though gossipers may make sport of me, though brothers may jealously despise me, I will celebrate! Let all hear music and dancing! For I once was dead and now I'm alive again. I once was lost and now I am found.

What are your usual reactions and responses to the prodigals you know? Do they receive your love and fervent prayer? Or is there resistance in your eyes? What would you like them to know about the love of God, and how could you show it to them? _____

_____

_____

_____

_____

_____

_____

_____

Praying God's Word Today

Lord, when we were dead in trespasses and in the uncircumcision of our flesh, You made us alive with You and forgave us all our sins. You erased our certificate of debt, with all its obligations—everything that was against us and opposed to us. You have taken it out of the way by nailing it to the cross (Col. 2:13–14). While we were still sinners, You died for us (Rom. 5:8). May I never grow too familiar with this truth not to recognize its enormity.

DAY 64

Whose Fault Is It?

Before You Begin
Read Matthew 18:1–9

Stop and Consider
Woe to the world because of offenses. For offenses must come,
but woe to that man by whom the offense comes. (v. 7).

What relationships or activities in your life are least conducive to holy living? In which
ones do you find yourself most likely to be compromised or taken advantage of? _____

_____

_____

What are your best defenses against being manipulated or lured into sin? _____

_____

_____

_____

_____

Let's state a serious fact based on Matthew 18: events or situations can actually cause people to sin. Before we attempt to interpret Christ's statements, let's make sure we understand what He didn't mean. Christ didn't mean that in some cases people have no choice *but* to sin. He didn't absolve the one who sins from the responsibility to repent. He did mean, however, that conditions can exist and things can happen that so greatly increase the tendency toward sin that a terrible woe is due the responsible party.

What are these offenses or "things that cause people to sin"? (Luke 17:1). The Greek word is *skandalon*. The idea of our English word "scandal" is present in the meaning. *Skandalon* is "the trigger of a trap on which the bait is placed, and which, when touched by the animal, springs and causes it to close, causing entrapment. It always denotes an enticement to conduct which could ruin the person in question."

If you apply this concept to Jesus' words, you see that the declaration of "woe" would apply to the one who set the trap or (figuratively speaking) became the trigger of the trap. But to be liberated we must not shift all responsibility to the trapper, because the truth remains that we did take the bait. To live consistently outside a trap, we must recognize our own responsibility in at least three ways. We are responsible for:

1) *repenting of the sin* of taking the bait;

2) *learning why* we took the bait;

3) *asking God* to mend and fortify the weak places in the fabric of our heart, soul, and mind so we will not continue life as a victim.

A critical part of my own personal freedom in Christ has been asking God to help me search my heart, soul, and mind for vulnerabilities to foolish decisions. Taking responsibility in these areas produced one of the greatest harvests of my life. I learned to willingly lay my heart bare before Him, to invite Him to reveal my weaknesses and handicaps, and to be unashamed. I also developed daily dependency upon Him because my old vulnerabilities had become such habits, practices, and ways of life.

This doesn't minimize, of course, the sin of the trapper. The ramifications of this are so great that he becomes the object of "woe," meaning "disaster, calamity." Christ issued a woe to anyone who causes another person to sin, but He pronounced a particular indictment against anyone who causes "one of these little ones" to sin (v. 6).

The word Jesus used to refer to "little ones" certainly includes literal children, because He actually "called a little child and had him stand among them" (Matt. 18:2). However, careful attention to the word suggests additional meaning. I believe Christ includes those who are childlike or inferior to the trapper in knowledge, experience, authority, or power—anyone of whom it might be easy to take advantage. A sixteen-year-old may have the body of an adult, but he or she most assuredly is not grown up. Seduction by an adult is entrapment even if the young person "sinned" in any level of willing participation. Similarly, in adult life, one person often wields authority over another in much the same way through rank or position.

> No trapper gets away with entrapment forever— either of the human kind or the spirit kind. No one can escape the eyes of El Roi, the God who sees.

That Christ holds the trapper greatly responsible is a gross understatement! He appears to be saying, "If you have entrapped a weaker, more vulnerable person in sin, you're going to wish you had drowned in the deepest sea rather than deal with Me."

Most of us have asked, "Why do these things happen?" Matthew 18:7 tells us that these atrocities "must come." "But why?" we ask. The original word for "must" means "compelling force, as opposed to willingness. As a result of the depravity and wickedness of men, there is a moral inevitability that offenses should come." Add the kingdom of darkness to the depravity of humans, and you have a formula for exactly the evil we see in our world. But a day of reckoning is coming. No trapper gets away with entrapment forever—either of the human kind or the spirit kind. Neither can escape the eyes of *El Roi*, the God who sees.

Most of us are not naïve enough to think that these kinds of offenses never happen in churchgoing families. I'd like to highlight one area that doesn't get much press but where people are at great risk for offense in the church: New believers are so impressionable. Sometimes their zeal far exceeds their knowledge. They sometimes believe virtually anything a more experienced Christian tells them. Biblical doctrines can be twisted into false teaching to entrap immature believers in all sorts of sins. If God would judge those outside His own household, I think we can rest assured He would discipline His own.

Let's not start feeling guilty for some atrocity we may not have committed, but by all means let's be on our guard never to cause another person to sin. The Word is clear we have that potential.

Is it possible that you're creating an environment—at home, at work, at church, in your friendships—that is causing another person to sin? How could you put a stop to this?

Praying God's Word Today

O Father, I know that I must be careful not to become a stumbling block to others, for when I sin against my brothers and sisters and wound their consciences, I am really sinning against You (1 Cor. 8:9, 12). Protect me, Lord, from either willingly or unwillingly harming even one of Your children. I desire to be a blessing, not an obstacle. _____

DAY 65

*The Fine Art
of Forgiveness*

Before You Begin
Read Luke 17:3–4

Stop and Consider

If he sins against you seven times a day, and comes back to you
seven times, saying, "I repent," you must forgive him (v. 4).

Why did Jesus make forgiveness such a strong command, even when human logic would
tell you that "seven times a day" is an impossible directive to follow? _____

_____

_____

Are we biblically allowed to put some "teeth" in our forgiveness? Is forgiveness anything
other than a total, free pass? _____

_____

_____

_____

After dealing with the subject we talked about yesterday—things that cause people to sin—Christ suddenly switched to a subject that seems to have no relationship to this. I'd like to suggest, however, a powerful connection between the two. Few things cause people to sin like unforgiveness. Difficult-to-forgive circumstances can set a trap. And Satan is very adept at using unforgiveness as bait to entrap us in sin (2 Cor. 2:10–11).

Please note that Christ's specific prescriptive in Luke 17:3–4 is to fellow believers when we sin against one another. Someone might ask, "Does this mean I have to forgive only other Christians?" No, indeed. Luke 11:4 clearly tells us we are to forgive "everyone" who sins against us. The difference may not be in the forgiveness but in the rebuke. I believe Christ suggests a different method of dealing with a brother's or sister's sin. He issued a directive to "rebuke" a fellow believer (v. 3). When dealing with the unsaved, we are still called to forgive—but not necessarily to rebuke.

We were called to be different in the body of Christ. If we are functioning as a healthy body, ideally we should be able to bring issues that affect us to the table with one another to dialogue and, when appropriate, even to rebuke or receive a rebuke. This type of approach demands the maturity expressed by Ephesians 4:14–15. Paul told us we are no longer to be infants but are to "speak the truth in love" to one another.

Needless to say, a tremendous burden of responsibility falls on the one *giving* the rebuke. An appropriate rebuke is speaking the truth in love "with great patience and careful instruction" (2 Tim. 4:2). We may not be off base in concluding that a rebuke which invites anger and bitterness might fall under the category of entrapment to sin. Obviously, a huge responsibility also falls on the recipient to rightly *accept* the rebuke. I am learning that an important part of maturing as a believer is knowing how to receive a rebuke.

If we would learn the art of giving and receiving an appropriate rebuke in the early stages of wrongdoing, we would guard ourselves more effectively against offenses of "millstone" magnitude (Luke 17:2). I don't know about you, but I'll be chewing on this lesson long into the night.

PRAYING GOD'S WORD TODAY

Lord, You teach us very early in Your Word, "You must not hate your brother in your heart. Rebuke your neighbor directly, and you will not incur guilt because of him. Do not take revenge or bear a grudge against members of your community, but love your neighbor as yourself" (Lev. 19:17–18). As one who has received such immeasurable forgiveness through the blood of Christ, may I be more than willing to forgive those who sin against me—and to care enough about them to lead them to life.

DAY 66

Return to Glory

BEFORE YOU BEGIN

Read Luke 17:11–19

STOP AND CONSIDER

Jesus said, "Were not 10 cleansed? Where are the nine?
Didn't any return to give glory to God except this foreigner?" (vv. 17–18).

How have you worn shame wrapped around your shoulders? It may not be as obvious as the
way these lepers carried themselves in tatters. But do you feel "unclean" nonetheless? _____

_____

_____

What would deliverance and healing look like on you? _____

_____

_____

_____

_____

While I ministered in India, I was often stunned by what God empowered me to do. He seemed to raise me above my fleshly senses and allow me to minister in extreme circumstances. Only one thing was I unable to do, and it has haunted me ever since. I had confidently planned to minister in a leper colony. The opportunity didn't readily arise, but after passing very close to several colonies, I deliberately did not pursue it.

The reason was not unconcern. Rather, I feared I would dishonor them by becoming physically ill. I almost became ill just passing by. Nothing could have prepared me for the sight or the smell. I had been in one squalid village after another without hindrance, but the smell of diseased and decaying flesh was more than I could handle.

I don't know if God was upset with me, but I was definitely upset with myself. My experience helps me to appreciate this story. Let's highlight several significant pieces of information shared about the lepers in Luke 17.

1) The lepers were outside the city gate. What could be worse than forced isolation? I can hardly stand the thought of the emotional results of this dreadful disease, especially in an ancient society. The law of Moses said, "As long as he has the infection he remains unclean. He must live alone; he must live outside the camp" (Lev. 13:46).

Try to imagine what this was like. Oh, beloved, I'm so grateful we never have to stand at a distance from Christ. Not only is He incapable of catching our "disease," He is never reluctant to embrace us. Who could be more brokenhearted, more crushed in spirit, than these outcasts? Yet in the words of Psalm 34:18, "The LORD is close to the brokenhearted and saves those who are crushed in spirit." He drew near them with His soothing balm.

2) The lepers cried out in a loud voice. Don't miss the fact that every word attributed to the lepers is in a "loud voice" (vv. 13, 15). The distance explains their initial volume, but why did the one who returned and fell at Jesus' feet also cry out in a loud voice?

I'd like to suggest that they were accustomed to having to shout. Leviticus 13:45 is probably as hard for you to read as it is for me: "The person with such an infectious disease must wear torn clothes, let his hair be unkempt, cover the lower part of his face and cry out, 'Unclean, unclean!'"''

Because of the nature of this ministry and my own testimony, I encounter many people who live like the ten lepers. They are in bondage either to sin or to the aftereffects of sin. Their voices may be silent, but their expressions cry out: "Unclean! Unclean!" They feel excluded from the pretty part of the body of Christ. Yet they feel their shame is displayed for all to see. My heart breaks every time. These lepers were not just asking for sympathy. They needed someone to change their lives, and Jesus was the One and Only who could.

> Christ still overflows today with a pity that doesn't just sympathize but changes conditions. Often physically. Always spiritually.

3) The common condition of the lepers eclipsed their differences. The lepers had to have been a mix of Samaritans and Jews. Christ never would have commented that only a "foreigner" returned with thanks if none of the ten had been Jews. Yet the tragic plight of the lepers gave them far more in common with each other than their differences as Jews and Gentiles. Aren't we the same way? Before we are redeemed, not one of us is better than the other. We are all in the same sad state—lepers outside the city gate. Lost and isolated. Marred and unclean—whether we've lied or cheated, devalued another human being, or committed adultery. Lost is lost. Furthermore, found is found. All of us in Christ have received the free gift of salvation in one way only: grace. When we judge a brother's or sister's sin as so much worse than our own, we are like lepers counting spots.

4) The lepers were cleansed during their faith-walk to the priest. I love the way Scripture refers to their healing as being made clean (v. 14). Oh, dear sister or brother, that's what healing has meant to me. Being made clean! Do you know why I recognize those who wear shame like a cloak? Scarlet letters on their chests? Because I did. But I don't anymore. Acts 10:15 tells us so clearly, "Do not call anything impure that God has made clean."

You can be fairly certain the village priest had never practiced the purification ritual to pronounce a leper clean. I can almost picture him reading the instructions in Leviticus 14 step by unfamiliar step—like we read a new recipe. What a story he had for the Mrs. that night! Then again, it wouldn't have been like a woman to miss the parade of ten former lepers dancing their way down Main Street. Finally, note the punch line of the event:

5) One leper returned to give praise to God. I wonder if he tried to get the other nine to come with him. Or if he suddenly stopped in his tracks realizing he hadn't said thanks, then darted impulsively from their presence to find Christ. The point is, his healing made him think of his healer, not just himself. Sadly, the rest of them never knew Christ except from a distance. When the one returned, he was unrestrained—falling at Christ's feet and thanking Him.

Just one last thought. I wonder if he was the one with the most spots?

Gratitude is more than just words, of course. What are a handful of ways you could "say" thanks to Him without speaking a syllable? _____

_____

_____

_____

_____

_____

_____

Praying God's Word Today

Lord Jesus, You have given us confidence to declare that nothing can separate us from Your love (Rom. 8:39). You have given us the bold assurance that we will not be ashamed before You at Your coming (1 John 2:28). You have said, in fact, that we have been cleansed already through the Word that You have spoken to us (John 15:3). May we truly take You at Your Word, and respond to You with lives of loving gratitude. _____

_____

_____

_____

_____

_____

_____

_____

_____

_____

_____

DAY 67

*Too Good for
Your Own Good?*

Before You Begin
Read Luke 18:18–21

Stop and Consider
"I have kept all these from my youth," he said (v. 21).

Did you live a fairly straight-laced childhood? How much stock do you think you've put in that fact whenever you've measured yourself on the "goodness" meter? _____

_____

_____

There's certainly nothing the least bit disrespectable about a holy, separated life. It sure beats the alternative! But how do you keep it from becoming a pride issue? _____

_____

_____

_____

_____

Consider the abbreviated list of commandments Christ mentioned—each of which concerned man's relationship with man—and then let's play a game together. Take a look at each command the ruler claimed to have kept since boyhood. Give each a mental check mark for his probable obedience, or a mental X for those that seem a little less probable.

• *"Do not commit adultery."* Okay, this one may have been a pretty easy check mark—that is, if he knew nothing about lust being the same thing as committing adultery in his heart (Matt. 5:27–28). Let's give him a check mark here.

• *"Do not murder."* Of course, there's that little "anger" issue that Christ discussed in Matthew 5:21–22, but let's go ahead and give him a check mark on this one, too.

• *"Do not steal."* Maybe we've never mugged someone on the street or even swiped candy from the convenience store, but did we ever secretly defraud or steal anything of a less tangible nature from another person? Perhaps so. I'm still willing to give him a check mark, but let me just say I'm impressed!

• *"Do not give false testimony."* This command is simple: never tell anything false or untrue. Any exaggeration would fall under the category of false testimony. Picture us at age seventeen, talking to our friends on the telephone, giving our version of this story and that. The rich young ruler's protection may have been that he had never been a seventeen-year-old girl nor owned a phone. Hopefully he never had time to fish either. We can give him a check mark if he insists, but you better give me an X.

• *"Honor your father and mother."* Let's see. I hardly ever dishonored mine to their faces, but does it count if, behind their backs, I did a few things they told me not to do? Oops. Go ahead and give the wonder boy a check mark, but I get another X.

How did you fare? Shall we call you perfection personified? Or is your halo slipping a bit? As for me, am I thankful for a Savior! The rich young ruler needed one too. His good track record had certainly fogged up his mirror. Don't get me wrong. I like him. I'm even impressed with him, but I'd rather be saved than be like him!

PRAYING GOD'S WORD TODAY

Lord Jesus, I know that You created me for good works, which You prepared ahead of time so that I would walk in them. But I am more aware than ever each day that it is by Your grace I have been saved through faith—not from works, so that I have no reason to boast (Eph. 2:8–10). May I never boast in anything except the cross of Christ, through which the world has been crucified to me, and I to the world (Gal. 6:14). _____

_____

_____

_____

_____

_____

_____

_____

_____

_____

_____

DAY 68

Money Troubles

Before You Begin
Read Luke 18:22–30

Stop and Consider
When Jesus heard this, He told him, "You still lack one thing: sell all that you have and distribute it to the poor, and you will have treasure in heaven. Then come, follow Me" (v. 22).

How many ways can money work its way into your affections? _____

_____

_____

Which of these have been the most acute in your own life? Which ones have required the most effort on your part to maintain victory over their seductive tendencies? _____

_____

_____

_____

If this were a game show, the bell indicating the mention of the secret word would have just sounded. Eternal life with God demands perfection. Someone has to be perfect. Either us or someone who stands in for us. This man wanted so badly for it to be him. But as good as he had been and as hard as he had tried, he was still lacking. Christ then stuck a pin in the rich young ruler's Achilles' heel: his possessions.

One of the primary purposes of this divine pinprick was to show the man he wasn't perfect nor would he ever be. I really believe a second purpose may have been to offer an authentic invitation for the searching young man to follow Him. Remember, Jesus didn't have only twelve disciples. He had twelve *apostles* among a greater number of disciples. If the rich young ruler had done what Christ suggested, could he have followed Him? Certainly! He simply needed to lighten his load and be free of wealth's encumbrances. A truckful of possessions would have proved cumbersome.

I also believe Christ had a purely benevolent purpose for the seemingly harsh demand. Jesus looked at this young man and saw a prisoner. The man wasn't really the ruler. His possessions were. Jesus pointed him to the only path to freedom. Sometimes when our possessions have us, we have to get rid of them to be free.

Of course, Christ knew in advance what the young man would choose. When it comes right down to it, we all follow our "god." The ironic part about this story, however, is that the rich young ruler was grief stricken over his own choice. He walked away very sad or in Greek, *perilupos*: "severely grieved, very sorrowful." Unless his heart changed somewhere along the way, he lived the rest of his life with all that wealth and an empty heart. The question would have haunted him forever: "What do I still lack?" (Matt. 19:20).

Perfection or a perfect substitute. He had neither. He lacked Jesus.

I wonder if the man stuck around long enough to hear the rest of the conversation between Christ and His disciples (vv. 24–30). Jesus said something like: "Yes, an eternal inheritance involves sacrifice here on earth, but whatever you lay down here for My sake, you will receive a hundred times as much in eternity." How sad to believe anything less.

Praying God's Word Today

Father, please help me guard against setting my hopes on the uncertainty of wealth, but rather on You, who richly provide us with all things to enjoy. Help me to be rich in good works, to be generous, willing to share, storing up for myself a good foundation for the days to come, so that I may take hold of life that is real (1 Tim. 6:17–19). _____

_____

_____

_____

_____

_____

_____

_____

_____

_____

_____

_____

_____

_____

DAY 69

Little Man
Makes Big News

Before You Begin
Read Luke 19:1–10

Stop and Consider

When Jesus came to the place, He looked up and said to him,
"Zacchaeus, hurry and come down, because today I must stay at your house" (v. 5).

How many times does Jesus have to call before you respond to His invitation? What makes a person more willing to move quickly when His Word is proclaimed? _____

_____

_____

What has He been inviting you to do with Him lately? _____

_____

_____

_____

_____

Can you imagine what the title of the next day's headline would have been if there had been a newspaper called *The Jericho Chronicle*? As a means of creative exploration, let's try to capture a few of the newsiest statements that might have appeared in their morning editions. The lead story might have read:

• *The Renowned Jesus of Nazareth Passes through Jericho.* Jesus couldn't seem to pass through anywhere without getting involved. He seemed to attract the dust of every village in His sandals no matter how resolved He was to reach Jerusalem. I wonder if His disciples were ever frustrated that He couldn't go anywhere without encountering one commotion after another. I'm sure His followers were thrilled and amazed by all He did, but I'm also sure they were often tired, hungry, and famished—and wouldn't have minded going unnoticed every once in a while.

• *Chief Tax Collector Seen Scurrying Up Tree.* Zacchaeus wanted to see Jesus so badly, he went to considerable lengths for a grown man. Picture him running ahead of the parade of people, looking for a tree with a view. Did he have to jump to reach a sturdy branch, or did the sycamore spare him a nice, low rung? Can you hear him huffing and puffing his way up that tree? Clad in a robe, no less? Nothing like climbing a tree in a long dress. How long has it been since you climbed your last tree?

• *Traveling Man Requests Chief Publican's Hospitality.* I can almost picture Christ working His way through the crowd as if totally oblivious to the short man in a tall tree. He suddenly looked up with complete familiarity. "Zacchaeus," He said. How in the world did Jesus know his name? Maybe the same way He knew Nathaniel's a few years earlier. "Zacchaeus, come down immediately. I must stay at your house today" (Luke 19:5). Why must He? Perhaps because the Son lived to do the will of His Father, and His Father simply could not resist a display of interest in His Son. The Father and Son have an unparalleled mutual admiration society. That day Zacchaeus may have had a pair of skinned knees and elbows that endeared a special dose of the Father's affections.

Luke 19:6 says, "So he came down at once and welcomed him gladly." At once. I'm not sure God honors anything more in a man than a timely response to His Son. No doubt the chief tax collector had many regrets in life, but among them wasn't the time he wasted between Christ's invitation and his welcome.

> God carefully knitted those short legs of a certain tax collector, knowing that one day he'd use them to scurry up a sycamore tree to see His Son.

• *Chief Publican Caught in the Act of Rejoicing.* I don't think we're off base to imagine that his sudden display of glee was slightly out of character. The Word doesn't paint tax collectors as campus favorites. Don't you love how Christ can change an entire personality? Not only can He make the blind man see, but He can also perform a much greater feat: He can make the grump rejoice! Our church pews might not have so many empty seats if we'd invite Him to display such a feat in us! The good news coming from people in a bad mood undermines the message a tad.

Don't you think Christ delights in our glad responses, when we rejoice to obey Him? Let me be clear that God honors obedience even when we're kicking and screaming. But can you imagine how blessed He is when we're eager to do His will?

• *Noted Preacher Goes to Dinner with Sinner.* I think you'll enjoy the definition of the Greek word for "guest" in Luke 19:7. The word means "to loose or unloose what was before bound or fastened. To refresh oneself, to lodge or be a guest. It properly refers to travelers loosening their own burdens or those of their animals when they stayed at a house on a journey." In effect, Zacchaeus's hospitality said to Jesus: "Come to my house and take a load off. Lay Your burden down and be refreshed. I'd be honored to have You." What an awesome thought that at the same time, Christ was saying to Zacchaeus: "Let Me come into your house and take your load. Lay your burden down and be refreshed. I'd be honored to have you."

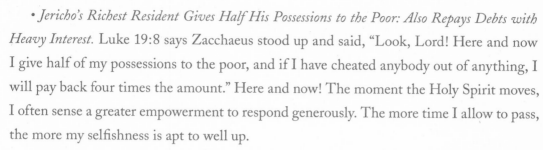

• Jericho's Richest Resident Gives Half His Possessions to the Poor: Also Repays Debts with Heavy Interest. Luke 19:8 says Zacchaeus stood up and said, "Look, Lord! Here and now I give half of my possessions to the poor, and if I have cheated anybody out of anything, I will pay back four times the amount." Here and now! The moment the Holy Spirit moves, I often sense a greater empowerment to respond generously. The more time I allow to pass, the more my selfishness is apt to well up.

One short man had never stood taller than he did on this day. I don't hear a single shred of resistance, do you? He almost seemed anxious to get rid of some things. Perhaps the wealth had been less a blessing and more a curse. Proverbs 15:27 tells us, "A greedy man brings trouble to his family, but he who hates bribes will live." Maybe Zacchaeus had come to see the trouble of valuing wealth over God.

Either way, it was a big news day in Jericho . . . and for the little guy in the headlines.

What is the most marked difference Jesus Christ has made in your life, whether in your overall demeanor or in a specific life practice? _____

_____

_____

_____

_____

_____

_____

PRAYING GOD'S WORD TODAY

Father, how grateful I am that when we come to our senses—when we repent and petition you, saying "We have sinned and done wrong; we have been wicked"—when we return to You with our whole mind and heart in the land where the enemy has taken us captive—when we pray to You—You hear us in heaven, Your dwelling place. You uphold our cause and forgive our sins. For we are Your people and Your inheritance (1 Kings 8:47–51). How can we praise You enough for such love and compassion? _____

_____

_____

_____

_____

_____

_____

_____

_____

DAY 70

The Choice to Change

BEFORE YOU BEGIN

Read Hebrews 10:32–39

STOP AND CONSIDER

We are not those who draw back and are destroyed,

but those who have faith and obtain life" (v. 39).

What were the real differences between these two men we've looked at lately: Zacchaeus and the rich young ruler? _____

_____

_____

Quickly profile an example of someone you know who hasn't drawn back from following, even against significant obstacles. What do you love most about this person's testimony?

_____

_____

_____

I don't remember a whole lot about my life before salvation, because I was very young. But I can tell you that Christ's authority over my life has dramatically changed both my demeanor and life practices. I was once overly sensitive and very fearful. I would ten times rather have watched television than studied His Word. My character showed it too. Oh, I have a long way to go; but change is not only possible, it's also gloriously inevitable, "being confident of this, that he who began a good work in you [and in me] will carry it on to completion until the day of Christ Jesus" (Phil. 1:6).

I have waited until now to ask you to reflect on some words of Jesus from a previous story we read of the rich young man, so that we can compare this guy with Zacchaeus. Please observe Luke 18:24–25: "How hard it is for the rich to enter the kingdom of God! Indeed, it is easier for a camel to go through the eye of a needle than for a rich man to enter the kingdom of God."

A rich young ruler. A chief publican. Both wealthy men. One walked away lost, while salvation lodged at the other's home. Salvation was not impossible for either one of these rich men. Both had the Son of God standing right there in front of them . . . willing and able to deliver. The difference was that one saw how much he had to lose. The other saw how much he had to gain.

Notice, Christ did not ask Zacchaeus to sell everything he had and give to the poor, as He did to the younger man. Maybe because once Zacchaeus regarded Christ as life's true treasure, his wealth didn't mean nearly as much to him—which I believe is probably God's primary point to the rich.

A cynic might say, "Why did he only give away half to the poor?" Maybe because it took every other shekel to pay back all the folks he had cheated! Anyway, God isn't looking to take away our possessions. He is looking to make His Son our greatest possession.

"My righteous one will live by faith. And if he shrinks back, I will not be pleased with him" (Heb. 10:38). If you're facing a choice right now between pressing forward and drawing back, look at these two men. Which one do you want to be more like?

Praying God's Word Today

Lord God, I'm inspired by the life of Your servant Moses, who chose to live with (even to suffer with) the people of God rather than to enjoy the short-lived pleasures of sin. For he considered reproach for the sake of Christ to be greater wealth than the treasures of Egypt, because his attention was on his reward (Heb. 11:25–26). When my endurance fails, Lord, would you help me keep focusing on the great reward of Your favor and eternal promises? I don't want to slow down or lose sight. I want to keep going. Please help me, Lord.

DAY 71

Unmistakable

Before You Begin
Read Luke 21:5–28

Stop and Consider
When these things begin to take place, stand up and lift up

your heads, because your redemption is near! (v. 28).

What are some of your biggest questions about Christ's Second Coming? What would you
love to know the answer to? _____

_____

_____

Is it fair to ask questions like these—even if we may never receive the answer? Is it possible
for a person to ask in curiosity and believe in faith all at the same time? _____

_____

_____

_____

I love eschatology—a fancy word for end-time events. Few subjects are more exciting to study than the glorious future awaiting us. Just don't lose your head over it! Bible topics are not meant to become our focus—not even critical themes like holiness and service. *Jesus* is our focus. Remember, the enemy's primary goal is to disconnect us from the Head. Colossians 2:19 describes the kind of person who becomes more interested in spiritual things than the Spirit of Christ: "He has lost connection with the Head." That's why we must be very careful when dealing with exciting subjects like eschatology.

Among the many facts we know about Christ's return, the one that is most clear is this one: *it will be unmistakable.* Luke 21:27 tells us that people "will see the Son of Man coming in a cloud with power and great glory."

Revelation 1:7 also makes it clear that Christ's return to this earth will be impossible to miss: "Look, he is coming with the clouds, and every eye will see him, even those who pierced him; and all the peoples of the earth will mourn because of him. So shall it be! Amen."

If you carefully compare Luke 21:7 with Matthew 24:3, you will see that the disciples asked about Jesus about two events. I believe the disciples thought they were asking only one question. In reality they asked about two events separated by millennia—the destruction of the temple and the return of Christ. The temple was destroyed in 70 A.D. We await Jesus' return today.

I confess that I would like to shake those disciples and tell them to ask better questions. Parts of Jesus' discourse fit the events surrounding the destruction of the temple. Some of His words can apply only to the Second Coming. Some leave us wondering. Why do you suppose Jesus didn't choose to be more clear about these events? Wouldn't you like to have a clearer road map or timetable?

But whether or not we can answer all the questions that come to our mind, you and I can be sure we are living in an era on the kingdom calendar that will climax with the visible return of Jesus Christ. It's unmistakable.

PRAYING GOD'S WORD TODAY

Alpha and Omega, the First and the Last, the Beginning and the End, I know that You are coming quickly, and that Your reward is with You to repay each person according to what he has done (Rev. 22:12–13). This I know. And for this, I worship You . . . and wait for You.

DAY 72

Things to Watch For

Before You Begin
Read Luke 17:20–36

Stop and Consider
As the lightning flashes from horizon to horizon and lights
up the sky, so the Son of Man will be in His day (v. 24).

What troubles you the most about the direction of our world and society? _____

_____

_____

What claims have you heard people proclaiming or broadcasting about the "end times" and
the "latter days" that you just know are not based on God's Word? _____

_____

_____

_____

_____

Let's emphasize a few facts concerning the end of the age and Christ's return:

1) Christians will long for Christ's return before the world ever sees it. Luke 17:22 intimates that one of the signs of His return will be a heightened longing. Christ is most assuredly returning, but not as soon as believers may hope as they look upon the tragic state of the earth. I experience that longing every time I watch a documentary on a starving, suffering people group or hear a horrific report of violence and victimization. My only answer is to pray, "O, Lord Jesus, come quickly!" I don't doubt that you also have overwhelming moments when you deeply long for Christ to return and right all wrongs.

2) Many will come claiming to be Christ. In Luke 17:23, Jesus warned that as the end of time hastens, the incidence of false-messiah claims will increase. But the sheer visibility of Christ's return is enough reason why believers should never be susceptible to this kind of deception. When Christ returns, people won't have to read about it in the paper. Every eye will see Him. Any rumor of His return is automatically false. When He comes back, the whole world will know it.

3) The world will display dramatic increases in depravity. One key word characterizing the hastening conclusion of this age is *increase*. God's Word describes end-time events like birth pains (see Matt. 24:8), meaning the evidences increase in frequency and strength. Matthew's version plainly characterizes the end of the age as marked by the increase of wickedness. "Because of the increase of wickedness, the love of most will grow cold" (Matt. 24:12).

Luke 17:25–28 states that the time of Christ's return will be like that of Noah or Lot. The Old Testament lends some important insight into the condition of the societies surrounding both of these men. I believe the end of time will parallel the days of Noah and Lot in many ways, but among them will be dramatic increase in perversity. Can anyone deny that we are living at a time of dramatic escalation in sexual sin? I believe our society is presently being sexually assaulted by the devil. I am convinced based on multiple characteristics of the last days that they have already begun. However, I'm certainly not date-setting Christ's return. Luke 12:40 makes it plain that forecasting a time of Christ's return is a waste of time. Jesus said, "the Son of Man will come at an hour when you do not expect him." So if we're going to be, like Noah, righteous people surrounded by a sea of unrighteousness, we have no other recourse than to radically refuse to cooperate and proactively choose to fight back. If we're going to be victorious in a latter-day society, we must become far more defensive and offensive in our warfare.

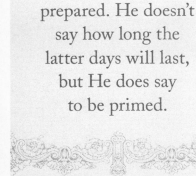

Christ doesn't want us date-setting, but He does want us prepared. He doesn't say how long the latter days will last, but He does say to be primed.

4) The latter days will show a notable increase in violence and cataclysmic events. Luke 21:10 tells us "nation will rise against nation, and kingdom against kingdom." Luke 21:12, 16 and Matthew 24:9 warn of the escalation in the persecution and martyrdom of Christians. Those of us who live in the United States like to think persecution and martyrdom are not characteristic of our generation of believers, but we are mistaken. Parts of our body are suffering terribly in many areas of the world.

Had enough bad news for now?

Me too! There's good news, too!

5) The worldwide witness of the gospel of Jesus Christ will increase. Ours is such a God of mercy! He will not judge the wickedness of the earth until the testimony of His Son has reached every nation. Jesus said, "The gospel of the kingdom will be preached in the whole world as a testimony to all nations, and then the end will come" (Matt. 24:14).

What kind of simultaneous increase does this prophecy necessitate? An increase in missionaries! Dr. Jerry Rankin of the Southern Baptist International Mission Board told me that the number of people surrendering to foreign missions is increasing so dramatically, it can be explained no other way than as God fulfilling prophecy. Rejoice in the fact that there will be a soul harvest that no man can count of every tribe, tongue, and nation (see Rev. 7:9)!

6) The activity of the Holy Spirit will increase. Acts 2:17 proclaims, "'In the last days, God says, I will pour out my Spirit on all people. Your sons and daughters will prophesy, your young men will see visions, your old men will dream dreams." I believe God was hinting at an insatiable appetite to know and share God's Word! Beloved, your love for Scripture is evidence of that harvest. We haven't simply "wised up" in this generation by getting into God's Word. It's the outpouring of the Holy Spirit! Unprecedented numbers of people are becoming armed with the sword of the Spirit because we're entering an unprecedented spiritual war!

I'm so grateful to live during this awesome season on the kingdom calendar. In some ways we live in the worst of times to date. But in other ways we live in the best of times. The winds of true worship are blowing. The Spirit of God is moving. I don't want to hold on to my church pew and sing, "I shall not be moved." I want to move with Him!

Don't you?

Pick one of these six points from today's devotional reading that really registered with you. What examples of it have you seen around you to prove God's Word is absolutely true?

_____

_____

_____

_____

_____

_____

Praying God's Word Today

Lord Jesus, I assure You—as Paul instructed us—that I am "encouraged" by the fact that You Yourself will one day descend from heaven with a shout, with the archangel's voice, and with the trumpet of God, and the dead in Christ will rise. Then those who are alive will be caught up together with them to meet You in the air; and so we will always be with You—all of us (1 Thess. 4:16–18). Lord, even though we haven't yet seen that great day, we know we are already safe within Your covenant love. Even so—come, Lord Jesus.

DAY 73

Beginning of the End

BEFORE YOU BEGIN

Read Luke 19:28–48

STOP AND CONSIDER

Every day He was teaching in the temple complex. The chief priests, the scribes,
and the leaders of the people were looking for a way to destroy him (v. 47).

Try to describe the emotions that flood your soul—after having spent these first seventy days
getting to know our One and Only—now seeing Him marked for a torturous death?

_____

_____

What could you do to keep the reality of His suffering and the high cost of your atonement
from ever becoming old hat and unmoving to you? _____

_____

_____

_____

We have arrived at the most critical juncture in our journey. Having accelerated through the parables, we now slow to a crawl, with magnifying glass in hand, to move through the final three chapters of Luke's Gospel. We will spend every remaining moment attempting to become eyewitnesses to the events at the conclusion of his account.

Luke 9:51 records that "Jesus resolutely set out for Jerusalem." He performed many miracles and delivered vital messages along the way. But Luke 19:28–48 indicates that Christ's presence was finally becoming more than His opposition could stand. His triumphal entry into Jerusalem, His cleansing of the temple. To the religious establishment, these were the proverbial straws that broke the camel's back.

I wish we could all sit together on the Mount of Olives and look at the Holy City for a while. Picture it in your mind. The garden where Christ retreated was on the hill directly across from the altar of sacrifice on the temple mount. Jesus taught at the temple during the day, then at night He retreated to the Mount of Olives, which overlooked the temple.

Not long ago, I sat near this place where Jesus retreated. I couldn't help wondering what went through His mind during those days. On that temple mount God had provided the substitutionary offering for Isaac (see Gen. 22:1–19; see also 2 Chron. 3:1). Paul wrote that through Abraham, God had provided an "advance" showing of the gospel of grace (Gal. 3:8). Fast forward, now, two thousand years to the scene where Christ was camped on the mountain parallel to the place of sacrifice at the temple. He resolved to fulfill the gospel that had been preached to Abraham. The time was imminent.

And, oh, by the way—"The Passover was approaching" (Luke 22:1). God's timing is never coincidental, but it was perhaps never more deliberate than in the events that unfolded in the opening lines of Luke 22. A new year on Israel's sacred calendar had just begun. The most sacred and critical year in all of human history was beginning—"the year of the Lord's favor" (Luke 4:19). The age of the completed redemptive work of God was unfolding. Can you imagine the anticipation in the unseen places? The kingdom of God and the kingdom of darkness were rising to a climactic point on the divine calendar.

PRAYING GOD'S WORD TODAY

Lord Jesus, how I praise You again for reconciling us by Your physical body through Your death, in order to present us holy, faultless, and blameless before You—if indeed we remain grounded and steadfast in the faith, and are not shifted away from the hope of the gospel we have heard and experienced (Col. 1:22–23). Please keep this reality before my eyes at all times, as I seek to worship You more fully each day.

DAY 74

Judas

Before You Begin

Read Luke 22:1–6

Stop and Consider

Then Satan entered Judas, called Iscariot, who was numbered among the Twelve.
He went away and discussed with the chief priests and temple police
how he could hand Him over to them (vv. 3–4).

Many people discount the work of Satan as the stuff of imagination and fairy tales. Why are you certain their doubts are misplaced? _____

_____

_____

What attention do you pay to him in your own life? How sure are you of his presence? How sure are you of Christ's victory over him? _____

_____

_____

_____

I wonder if Judas knew he was inhabited by Satan the moment it happened. Perhaps the entrance of the unholy spirit has counterfeit similarities to the entrance of the Holy Spirit. Most of us do not remember "feeling" the Holy Spirit take up residency within us the moment we trusted Christ as our Savior, yet He soon bore some sign of witness through the fruit in our lives. We have no way of knowing if Judas "felt" the unholy spirit take up residence within him, but it certainly wasn't long until the fruit of wickedness was revealed.

If you are new to the study of Scripture, the thought that Satan could enter a disciple might be terrifying. Please understand that just because a person appears to follow Christ doesn't necessarily mean he has placed saving faith in Him. Keep in mind that Satan entered Judas as opposed to Peter, James, or John, even though at times each of them had certainly revealed weakness of character. Satan was able to enter Judas because he was available. Judas followed Christ for several years without ever giving his heart to Him. The authentic faith of the others protected them from demon possession, albeit not oppression, just as it protects us. Judas proved to be a fraud, whether or not his tenure began with better intentions.

The evil one methodically seeks to work in your life and mine. Satan's planning counterfeits the awesome work of God. Just as our God has a holy plan that He executes in an orderly fashion, the enemy of our souls has an unholy plan he also executes in an orderly fashion.

Satan is not stupid. When I recall the technical procedures he's enacted in my life, I am stunned at his working knowledge of my fairly well-disguised vulnerabilities—even those I didn't know I had. He possesses a surprising amount of patience to weave seemingly harmless events into disasters, while his subject often never sees it coming.

What is our defense? The Word tells us not to be ignorant! Wising up to what the Word has to say about Christ's authority and the devil's schemes has empowered me to throw some holy kinks into Satan's unholy plans for my life.

PRAYING GOD'S WORD TODAY

O Father, may I realize my need today for putting on Your full armor so that I can stand against the tactics of the Devil. For I know my battle is not against flesh and blood, but against the rulers, against the authorities, against the world powers of this darkness, against the spiritual forces of evil in the heavens. But in You, Lord, I am strengthened by Your vast strength (Eph. 6:10–12). Praise the awesome and mighty name of the Lord!_____

DAY 75

Preparing the Lamb

Before You Begin
Read Luke 22:7–13

Stop and Consider

Jesus sent Peter and John, saying, "Go and prepare
the Passover meal for us, so we can eat it" (v. 8).

What task has Christ called you to lately, even though you're not crazy about doing it?

_____

_____

As you look at this specific activity again, what are some of the purposes you believe He
may be accomplishing in you as you faithfully live it out? _____

_____

_____

_____

_____

I don't believe Christ simply glanced up, saw Peter and John, and decided they'd be as good a choice as anyone to prepare for the Passover. Quite the contrary, this profound work was prepared in advance for them to do (see Eph. 2:10). It's likely the two men may have wished someone else had been chosen for the tasks, some of which were usually assigned to women. The Passover involved a fairly elaborate meal with a very specific setting. They may have grumbled, as we often do. Why? Because we may have no idea as to the significance of the work God has called us to do.

Give some thought to the preparations Peter and John made. You can read about the original Passover in Exodus 12:1–14. The meal involved three symbolic foods to be eaten during every observance: "meat roasted over the fire, along with bitter herbs, and bread made without yeast" (Exod. 12:8).

While every part of the meal was highly symbolic, it had no meaning at all without the lamb. The most important preparation Peter and John made was the procuring and preparing of the Passover lamb. The detailed preparation involving the lamb would soon be fulfilled in Jesus Christ, of course. They may not have grasped the significance of it at the time, but eventually they "got it."

Peter and John are the only two of the Twelve who were recorded referring to Jesus as the Lamb. Many years later Peter would write of Jesus that we were redeemed "with the precious blood of Christ, a lamb without blemish or defect. He was chosen before the creation of the world, but was revealed in these last times for your sake" (1 Pet. 1:19–20). For John's part, you can read Revelation 5 for what I think is the most majestic passage in Scripture about the Lamb of God.

Is it coincidence that only these two apostles wrote about Jesus as the Lamb? Not on your life. Christ's ultimate goal in any work He assigns to us is to reveal Himself, either through us or to us. The Holy Spirit used the tasks He assigned Peter and John that day to reveal to them the Lamb of God, to deeply engrave these images and remembrances in their minds. Beloved, the tasks God gives you are never trivial.

PRAYING GOD'S WORD TODAY

Lord, You have said in Your Word, "A man's heart plans his way, but the LORD determines his steps" (Prov. 16:9). So I submit my way to You today, Father, knowing that any suffering or inconvenience of this present time is not worth comparing with the glory that is going to be revealed to us (Rom. 8:18), as You reveal Yourself to us in the midst of our daily obedience.

DAY 76

The Last Supper

Before You Begin
Read Luke 22:14–22

Stop and Consider
He took bread, gave thanks, broke it, gave it to them, and said,
"This is My body, which is given for you. Do this in remembrance of Me" (v. 19).

Consider the full gamut of human feelings Christ must have experienced at this moment. List as many as come to mind. _____

_____

_____

Is dread a sin? Especially in view of the anticipation Jesus certainly must have felt on this night, what do you think He would say to you when you're in one of life's tightest spots?

_____

_____

_____

_____

When the hour came, Jesus and His apostles reclined at the table. The Passover was a celebration for families and those closest to them. Christ was surrounded by His closest family. They may have been weak, self-centered, and full of unfounded pride, but they were His. He desired to spend this time with them.

Capture this meal with your imagination. I think we've inaccurately pictured the last meal as moments spent over the bread and the wine. Christ and His disciples observed the entire Passover meal together. Then He instituted the new covenant, represented by the bread and the wine.

As they gathered around the table at sundown, Christ took the father role in the observance. Soon after they gathered, He poured the first of four cups of wine and asked everyone to rise from the table. He then lifted His cup toward heaven and recited the Kiddush, or prayer of sanctification, which would have included these words or something very close: "Blessed art Thou, O Lord our God, King of the universe, Who createst the fruit of the vine. Blessed art Thou, O Lord our God, Who hast chosen us for Thy service from among the nations . . . Blessed art Thou, O Lord our God, King of the universe, Who hast kept us in life, Who hast preserved us, and hast enabled us to reach this season."[8] This is very likely the blessing He recited in Luke 22:17.

If Christ and His disciples followed tradition, they took the first cup of wine, asked the above blessing, observed a ceremonial washing, and broke the unleavened bread. These practices were immediately followed by an enactment of Exodus 12:26–27. The youngest child at the observance asks the traditional Passover questions, provoking the father to tell the story of the exodus. Early church tradition cited John as the youngest apostle.[9] In all likelihood, John assumed the role of the youngest child in the family, asking the traditional questions that provoked Christ to tell the story of the Passover. Many scholars believe John may have been the one who asked the questions at the last supper because of his position at the table. John 13:23 tells us John was reclining next to Christ.

The four cups of wine served at the Passover meal represented the four expressions, or "I wills" of God's promised deliverance in Exodus 6:6–7. At this point in the meal, Christ poured the second cup of wine and narrated the story of Israel's exodus in response to the questions. Oh, friend, can you imagine? Christ, the Lamb of God, sat at their table and told the redemption story! He recounted the story as only He could have—and then, at the very next sundown—He fulfilled it! Oh, how I pray He will tell it again for all of us to hear when we take it together in the kingdom!

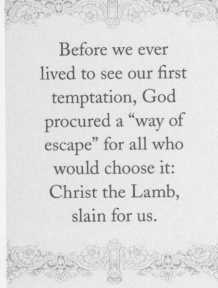

> Before we ever lived to see our first temptation, God procured a "way of escape" for all who would choose it: Christ the Lamb, slain for us.

They ate the meal between the second and third cups. Although all four cups would have been observed at the last supper, not all four cups are specified in Luke's Gospel. We know, however, exactly which cup is specified in Luke 22:20 because of its place of observance during the meal. The third cup was traditionally taken after the supper was eaten. It is represented by the third "I will" statement of God recorded in Exodus 6:6: "I will redeem you with an outstretched arm and with mighty acts of judgment."

This is the cup of redemption. I am convinced this cup is also the symbolic cup to which Christ referred only an hour or so later in the garden of Gethsemane when He asked God to "take this cup from me" (Luke 22:42). This was a cup of which He could partake only with outstretched arms upon the cross.

The imminent fulfillment of the cup of redemption signaled the release of the new covenant that would be written in blood. We know Christ did not literally drink this third cup because He stated in Luke 22:18 that He would not drink of another cup until the coming of the kingdom of God. Instead of drinking the cup, He would do something of sin-shattering significance. He would, in essence, become the cup and pour out His life for the redemption of man.

Christ never took anything more seriously than the cup of redemption He faced that last Passover supper. His body would soon be broken so that the Bread of life could be distributed to all who would sit at His table. The wine of His blood would be poured into the new wineskins of all who would partake. It was time's perfect night—a night when the last few stitches of a centuries-old Passover thread would be woven onto the canvas of earth in the shape of a cross. Sit and reflect.

> *O perfect Lamb of Passover,*
> *Let me not quickly run.*
> *Recount to me the blessed plot,*
> *Tell how the plan was spun*
> *That I, a slave of Egypt's lusts,*
> *A prisoner of dark dread,*
> *Could be condemned unto a cross*
> *And find You nailed instead.*

How do you "remember" the death of Christ at each observance of the Lord's Supper?

_____

_____

_____

_____

_____

PRAYING GOD'S WORD TODAY

O Lord Jesus, my heart nearly bursts hearing You say to Your Father, "You did not desire or delight in sacrifices and offerings, whole burnt offerings, and sin offerings. . . . See, I have come to do Your will." Lord, I know it is by this "will" that we have been sanctified through the offering of Your body, once and for all (Heb. 10:8–10). I humbly bow before You today, celebrating Your obedience to the Father and Your covenant love for me.

DAY 77

Still Teaching,
Still Learning

BEFORE YOU BEGIN
Read Luke 22:24–30

STOP AND CONSIDER

Who is greater, the one at the table or the one serving? Isn't it the one
at the table? But I am among you as the One who serves (v. 27).

How many lessons have you learned from Christ the first time He presented them? Why
is your answer (and mine) most likely "zero"? _____

_____

_____

In dealing with others—spouse, children, employees, friends—how willing are you to
absorb their failure more than once? _____

_____

_____

_____

Are you like me? Do you want to be made like Him—but more through His victories than His sufferings? Thankfully, we have a Savior who is willing to steadfastly walk with us even when we take three steps forward and two steps back. We'll see the colors of His willingness painted like a mural on the walls of the upper room.

If we often find ourselves in contrast to Jesus' perfect character, we're not so unlike His original disciples. Their inability at the Passover table to pinpoint who was the worst among them led to a dispute over who was the greatest. Had not Christ already dealt with them over this issue? However, being declared "guilty as charged" only condemns us. Left alone, it does nothing to change us. Like the apostles, we are slow to learn.

When we recognize that the disciples' sandals fit our feet, let's allow Christ to kneel in front of us, slip them off, and wash our feet. Oh, how we need Jesus to minister humility to us. Without it, He will vastly limit how much He ministers through us. John 13 tells us how Jesus laid aside His garments and washed the disciples' feet.

As effective as the lesson was, Christ still hadn't settled the issue of greatness. He knew that the matter was so critical that He would need to prove on a field trip what He had taught in class. I could kick myself for forcing lessons into field trips instead of learning them in the classroom, but I don't mind telling you, field trips are effective! I fear the lesson on greatness is rarely learned in the classroom alone.

Within hours, each of these disciples would encounter just how "great" they were. All would desert Christ and flee (see Matt. 26:56). However, the lesson taught and demonstrated in the upper (class)room, then confirmed during the field trip, would eventually "stick." Christ turned these eleven status-seekers into humble servants.

Again I find myself so amazed at the character of Christ. Just when we wouldn't have blamed Him if He had thrown water all over them, He washed their feet. And just when they argued over who was the greatest, He paid them their greatest compliment. Luke 22:28 records His words, "You are those who have stood by me in my trials."

Praying God's Word Today

I can't get away from the picture of You bowing before Your disciples and washing their feet. But help me also not be able to get away from Your following statement to them: "If I, your Lord and Teacher, have washed your feet, you also ought to wash one another's feet. For I have given you an example that you also should do just as I have done for you" (John 13:14–15). Show me those who need their feet washed today, and help me follow through.

_____

_____

_____

_____

_____

_____

_____

_____

_____

_____

_____

_____

_____

DAY 78

Sifted Like Wheat

BEFORE YOU BEGIN
Read Luke 22:31–34

STOP AND CONSIDER

Simon, Simon, look out! Satan has asked to sift you like wheat.
But I have prayed for you that your faith may not fail. And you,
when you have turned back, strengthen the brothers (vv. 31–32).

What have been some of your "sifting" times? _____

_____

_____

What kind of "chaff" or undesirable character did it reveal in you? And what kind of
"wheat" did you come out of it with? What did you learn that you'll never forget? _____

_____

_____

_____

As surely as Christ knew Judas would betray Him, He knew the rest of His disciples would desert Him. He knew every move each disciple would make. The implication from Luke 22 is that Satan asked to "sift" the disciples "as wheat" in verse 31, and that Christ specified Peter's own encounter in verse 32. I tend to think the Scriptures imply Christ permitted Satan to attack Peter with greater force than the others. If so, we might want to ask ourselves why. I believe these few verses intimate several reasons.

1) Peter was the natural leader among the disciples. Christ seemed to be singling him out as a leader in Luke 22:31 as He directed the statement concerning all the disciples (plural "you") to Peter: "'Simon, Simon, Satan has asked to sift [all of] you [disciples] as wheat.'" Very likely, Christ thought that Peter, as a leader among the disciples, could either take or needed the extra heat. I have a hunch both apply. Please be encouraged that Satan can't just presume to sift a believer like wheat. I believe this precedent suggests he must acquire permission from Christ. (Compare Job 1.) Christ will not grant the devil permission to do anything that can't be used for God's glory and our good—if we let it.

But those in critical positions like Peter aren't the only ones who can benefit from a good sifting. Please know, if ever I put on a shoe that fits, it would be this one. I, too, as a servant, badly needed a sifting. And I assure you, God was faithful to permit it. Being sifted like wheat is not your regular brand of temptation. It's an all-out onslaught by the enemy to destroy you and cause you to quit. It surfaces what you detest most in yourself and reveals the ugliness of self. Not everyone has or needs such an experience.

The horror of my sifting season remains as real as yesterday, but (I pray) so is the grain left behind. The method of sifting wheat is to put it through a sieve and shake it until the chaff, little stones, and perhaps some tares rise to the surface. The purpose is that the actual grain can be separated and ground into meal. Satan's goal in sifting is to make us a mockery by showing us to be all chaff and no wheat. Christ, on the other hand, permits us to be sifted to shake out the real from the unreal, the trash from the true. The wheat that proves usable is authentic grain from which Christ can make bread.

Praise Christ's faithful name! Satan turned Peter's field trip into a field day, but he still couldn't get everything about Peter to come up chaff. Satan's plan backfired. He surfaced some serious chaff, to be sure, but Christ let Peter have a good look at it. Then Christ blew the chaff away, took those remaining grains, and demonstrated His baking skills. But Christ had a few other reasons for allowing Peter to be sifted like wheat.

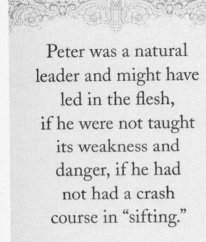

> Peter was a natural leader and might have led in the flesh, if he were not taught its weakness and danger, if he had not had a crash course in "sifting."

2) *Christ knew that Peter would turn back.* "But I have prayed for you, Simon, that your faith may not fail. And when you have turned back . . ." (Luke 22:32). Not *if*, but *when*. We're somewhat like books Satan can read only from the outside. His book review is limited to assumptions he makes about what's inside, based on what he reads on our "book jackets." He cannot read the inside of us as Christ can.

Satan observed Peter's overconfidence and propensity toward pride. He surmised that, when the sifting came, every page would come up chaff. He was wrong. Christ knew Peter's heart. He knew that underneath Peter's puffed-up exterior was a man with a genuine heart for God. Jesus knew that Peter could deny Christ to others, but he could not deny Christ to himself. He would be back—a revised edition with a new jacket.

3) *Christ knew how Peter's return and "revision" could be used for others.* "And when you have turned back, strengthen your brothers" (v. 32). From falling, Peter was about to learn how to stand. Peter would indeed fall, but his faith would not fail. He would use everything Christ taught him to strengthen his brothers.

Christ didn't want to take the leader out of Simon Peter. He just wanted to take Simon Peter out of the leader. His goal was to let Satan sift out all the Simon-stuff so Christ could use what was left: a humble jar of clay with no confidence in his flesh.

Not everyone has to learn to stand by falling. Better ways to learn exist, but I'm afraid that I learned a similar way. I finally learned to stand on Christ's two feet because my feet of clay turned out to be so unstable.

I was not so unlike Peter. I was young when I surrendered my life to Christ and was completely confident that nothing could shake my commitment. Excuse my bluntness, but I was an idiot. I cannot recall ever learning a more difficult lesson than that which my own sifting season taught me, but neither can I recall a lesson more deeply ingrained. Many years have passed, and I still do not live a day without remembering it and fearing another departure from Christ's authority more than I fear death.

I wouldn't wish a sifting on a single soul, but if that's what a life of harvest requires, may God use it so thoroughly that the enemy ends up being sorry he ever asked permission. Beloved, commitments can be shaken, but Christ cannot. When the shakedown comes, may the fresh winds of God's Spirit blow away the chaff until all that is left is the bread of life.

What does it do in your soul to know that Satan can't touch you without obtaining Christ's permission? And that when he does, Jesus has promised to pray for you?

PRAYING GOD'S WORD TODAY

You declare in Your Word, "Who can bring an accusation against God's elect? God is the One who justifies. Who is the One who condemns? Christ Jesus is the One who died, but even more, has been raised. He also is at the right hand of God and intercedes for us" (Rom. 8:33–34). Thank You, Lord Jesus, not only for knowing how much sifting I can stand, but also for being there with me, praying for me while I'm going through it. _____

_____

_____

_____

_____

_____

_____

_____

_____

_____

_____

DAY 79

Salvation's Song

BEFORE YOU BEGIN
Read Psalm 116:1–19

STOP AND CONSIDER
I will take the cup of salvation and worship the Lord. I will fulfill
my vows to the Lord in the presence of all His people (vv. 13–14).

What are some of the lines in your salvation song? What words or short phrases define
your experience with Christ? _____

_____

_____

What is the song of the unsaved like? What lines make up their life story? _____

_____

_____

_____

Tens of thousands of Jews celebrated the Passover that year in Jerusalem. For many, the year's observance was indistinct from the last. They had no idea that nearby the Lamb of God lifted the cup of redemption and offered it to all.

In the upper room the disciples' stomachs were full, their recollections rekindled, and their feet washed by the Son of man. "Having loved his own who were in the world, he now showed them the full extent of his love" (John 13:1). The One who created time submitted Himself to it. In the same perfect order that the heavens and the earth were created, salvation's story must unfold like a book already written . . . penned before the foundation of the world. The Spirit of God blew the next page open to the chapter called "Agony." The garden awaited.

"When they had sung a hymn, they went out to the Mount of Olives" (Matt. 26:30). Jesus singing! How I would love to hear that sound. When He sang, did the angels of heaven hush to His voice? Or did they cease their song and join in His? Did He sing tenor? Bass? Did Christ and His disciples sing in harmony, or did they all sing the melody? Did Jesus sing often, or was this a moment of rarity?

How fitting that on this very night Christ, the coming King, would give voice to songs penned centuries earlier just for Him. Traditionally, every Seder or Passover celebration ended with the latter half of the Hallel, Psalms 115–118. Very likely Christ and His disciples sang from these psalms. Imagine the Son of God singing these words as the seconds ticked toward the cross.

Whatever Christ sang as the Passover meal concluded that night, the words had significance for Him that the others could never have comprehended. I wonder if His voice quivered with emotion? Or did He sing with exultation? Perhaps He did both, just as you and I have done at terribly bittersweet moments when our faith exults while our sight weeps. One thing we know: Christ, above all others, knew that He was singing more than words. That night He sang the score of His destiny.

PRAYING GOD'S WORD TODAY

I will sing of Your strength, Lord Jesus—the strength I see in You again as I watch You face the cross and its suffering. I will joyfully proclaim Your faithful love in the morning. For You have been a stronghold for me, a refuge in my day of trouble. Therefore I sing praises to You, my strength. You are my stronghold, my faithful God (Ps. 59:16–17).

DAY 80

Please, Father

BEFORE YOU BEGIN
Read Mark 14:32–42

STOP AND CONSIDER

He said, "Abba, Father! All things are possible for You. Take this cup away from Me. Nevertheless, not what I will, but what You will" (v. 36).

What would you like to ask your Father to take off of your plate right now? _____

_____

_____

If He does, how deeply and publicly will you proclaim your praise for His mercy? If He doesn't, how faithfully will you follow Him through the valley with it? _____

_____

_____

_____

Without Mark's Gospel, we would not know Christ cried out to His Father using the name, "Abba." I don't often give you an extensive quote, but this one captured my soul with rich meditation; I hope it will yours.

> Abba is originally . . . a word derived from baby-language. When a child is weaned, "it learns to say 'abba (daddy) and 'imma (mummy)." . . . Also used by adult sons and daughters. . . . 'abba acquired the warm, familiar ring which we may feel in such an expression as "dear father." Nowhere in the entire wealth of devotional literature produced by ancient Judaism do we find 'abba being used as a way of addressing God. The pious Jew knew too much of the great gap between God and man to be free to address God with the familiar word used in everyday family life. . . . We find only one example of 'abba used in reference to God. It occurs in a story recorded in the Babylonian Talmud: "When the world had need of rain, our teachers used to send the schoolchildren to Rabbi Hanan ha Nehba [end of the 1st cent. B.C.], and they would seize the hem of his cloak and call out to him: 'Dear father ('abba), dear father ('abba), give us rain.' He said before God: 'Sovereign of the world, do it for the sake of these who cannot distinguish between an 'abba who can give rain and an 'abba who can give no rain.'"[10]

When Christ Jesus fell to His face and cried out, "Abba, Father," He cried out to the Abba who can give rain. The sovereign of the world was His Daddy. Everything was possible for Him . . . including removing the cup of dread.

Never minimize the moment by thinking God couldn't have removed the cup. Do not subtract God's freedom of choice from this picture. God could have chosen to reject the way of the cross. After all, He is the sovereign of the universe.

That God could have stopped the process yet didn't is a matchless demonstration of love. Can you think of anyone for whom you'd watch your only child be tortured to death? "'Abba, Father,' he said, 'everything is possible for you. Take this cup from me'" (Mark 14:36).

> Never minimize the moment by thinking God couldn't have removed the cup. That God could have stopped it yet didn't is a matchless demonstration of love.

The request Christ placed before the Father ought to make us catch our breath. It ascended to heaven through wails of grief. God's beloved was overwhelmed with sorrow to the point of death. Luke's Gospel tells us His sweat dropped like blood, a condition almost unheard of except when the physical body is placed in more stress and grief than it was fashioned to handle. Do we think God sat upon His throne unmoved?

Our hearts ought to miss a beat. Christ could have walked past the cross. He could have—but He didn't. Luke 22:47 tells us, "While he was still speaking a crowd came up." Imagine the scene they walked into that night.

Please try to grasp Christ's physical condition just before the crowd headed up the Mount of Olives to seize Him. Like a body that rejects a transplanted organ, the human body of Jesus Christ was practically tearing itself apart. The full throttle of divine impact and emotion was almost more than one human body could endure. The stress had nearly turned Him inside out. I do not make this point to emphasize His weakness. Quite the contrary. In fact I find the scene recorded in John 18:6 portrays His incredible power. When Jesus told the crowd, "I am he," even overwhelmed with sorrow to the point of death, the proclaimed presence of Jesus Christ knocked the mob to the ground.

Dear sweet Jesus. We really have no idea who You are, do we? Your God-ness could not be diminished for a moment, in or out of that prison of flesh. Lord, don't let us forget. You, who submitted Yourself to the hands of sinful men, were very God.

This seemed like another good place to give you ample room to journal your reflections, insights, and feelings. Because when you're not just glossing over Jesus' suffering but are letting it really soak in, the weight of it can be truly overwhelming. I invite you to pour out what you're experiencing right now. See the cost. Ponder what this means. _____

_____

_____

_____

_____

_____

_____

_____

_____

_____

_____

_____

_____

PRAYING GOD'S WORD TODAY

Like Paul, I would come to You with boldness, pleading for You to lift some of the heavy burdens I'm carrying right now. But in the midst of my request, I do hear you saying, "My grace is sufficient for you, for power is perfected in weakness." Therefore, I will most gladly boast all the more about my weaknesses, so that Your power, Lord Jesus, may reside in me. For when I am weak, then I am strong (2 Cor. 12:8–10). _____

_____

_____

_____

_____

_____

_____

_____

_____

_____

_____

_____

DAY 81

*A Serious Case
of Denial*

Before You Begin
Read Luke 22:47–62

Stop and Consider

Peter said, "Man, I don't know what you're talking about!"
Immediately, while he was still speaking, a rooster crowed (v. 60).

Followers of Christ can deny Him in other ways than Peter did. When have you suggested a similar denial by your actions, your words, or even your silence? _____

_____

_____

How has Jesus corrected you after episodes like these? What did His "look" feel like when you realized what you'd done? _____

_____

_____

_____

I am convinced that one reason God placed the account of Peter's denial in all four Gospels is so we'd sober to the reality that if Peter could deny Christ, any of us could. Never lose sight of the fact that Peter was certain he could not be "had." Yet he denied Christ not once. Not twice. But three times.

Denying Christ is huge. Do you think the blows Jesus later endured from the whip stung any more than Peter's denial? Don't minimize his sin in that courtyard. As we look at this again, I hope we'll recognize those factors that set Peter up for failure so we can avoid similar pitfalls.

1) Peter was willing to kill for Jesus, but he was reluctant to die for Him. Keep in mind the time element. Only an hour or so before Peter denied Christ to save his own skin, he had drawn a sword and cut off a man's ear. Maybe Peter's haste to use the sword was not just motivated by his desire to defend Jesus but by his concern to defend himself.

Nothing displays our self-love like a crisis. But Christ's disciples, both then and now, are called to live above that human baseline of self-importance. Remember that Christ had called Peter and His disciples to deny themselves and take up the cross daily (Luke 9:23). If Peter had denied himself, he would not have denied Christ.

The reason we can "forget" about ourselves is because Christ never forgets us. We can afford to be less important to ourselves because we are vastly important to God. Biblical self-denial will never fail to be *for* us rather than *against* us, whether here or in eternity. When Peter chose to deny Christ rather than himself, he really chose human limitations over divine intervention.

2) Peter followed Jesus, but at a distance. Obviously, if Peter had been holding onto Jesus' robe, he probably wouldn't have denied Him. Even though Christ asked the soldiers to let His disciples go (see John 18:8), why didn't even one insist upon staying, especially after all the miracles and proofs the Twelve had seen? From a divine standpoint the answer is most likely God's sovereignty in fulfilling prophecy that Christ would be deserted and forsaken. From a human standpoint, however, the answer is pure fear.

The scene reminds me of 2 Kings 2, when God was about to take His prophet, Elijah, up into a whirlwind. Elijah had several stops to make on his way to the Jordan River, and he continued his attempt to say farewell to his servant, Elisha. But all three times, Elisha said to him, "As surely as the LORD lives and as you live, I will not leave you" (2 Kings 2:2, 4, 6). If Peter had been as insistent as Elisha, Satan would not have had the room to come between him and his master with a sieve to sift him like wheat. Elisha's actions showed sheer determination to follow his master to the ends of his earthly life.

> Peter had to come face-to-face with the fact that in him, no good thing dwelled. Only then would he be willing to deny himself rather than Christ.

When we tiptoe to keep from being too obvious or to obscure ourselves in safe places and remain unidentifiable, we are already bounding toward denial.

3) Peter sat down with the opposition and warmed his hands by the same fire. I've been in Jerusalem in the early spring, so I can assure you the night was indeed cold. The semidesert climate may heat a spring day, but the temperature drops dramatically when the sun goes down. Since fear also has a way of quickening the senses, we're probably picturing Peter accurately as a young man who trembled nearly uncontrollably as he stood at that fire.

But I believe he made a very poor choice of company in the courtyard. John 18:18 tells us Peter joined "the servants and officials" at the fire in the middle of the courtyard. However unintentionally, he ended up surrounding himself with others who, in effect, denied Christ. The risk of failure heightened dramatically at that moment. Can we ever note a point of application here! Being sent by God to be a witness to those who "deny" Christ is one thing. Warming our hands by the same fire is another.

I cannot help but relate some of my own seasons of defeat to Peter's. I will regret some of my choices every day of my life. Like Peter, I also made some choices in my past that

went beyond rationalization. How thankful I am now that I couldn't just make excuses for my behavior! Any part of me I could have "excused" would still be "alive and kicking." Listen to my heart carefully: I want no part of myself. None. I want Jesus to so thoroughly consume me that I no longer exist. I am far too destructive. I would do far too much to deny His lordship. One regret I will never have is that God got me "over myself" by letting me confront this truth: in me dwells no good thing.

I do not doubt that Christ's face was painted with pain when His and Peter's eyes met in the courtyard, but I think the conspicuous absence of condemnation tore through Peter's heart. I wonder if Christ's fixed gaze might have said something like this: "Remember, Peter, I am the Christ. *You* know that and *I* know that. I called you. I gave you a new name. I invited you to follow Me. Don't forget who I am. Don't forget what you are capable of doing. And, whatever you do, don't let this destroy you. When you have turned back, strengthen your brothers."

The original language suggests that Peter took on every external form of grief. He wailed. He likely tore his clothes and threw handfuls of sand on his head. What have you learned from your spiritual failures, from times when you, too, "went outside and wept bitterly."

_____

_____

_____

_____

_____

PRAYING GOD'S WORD TODAY

Lord Jesus, I am chilled by Your statement, "Whoever denies Me before men, I will also deny Him before My Father in heaven." But as solemn and grievous as this warning is, I am even more in awe that You also say, "Everyone who will acknowledge Me before men, I will also acknowledge him before My Father in heaven" (Matt. 10:32–33). O Lord, what incredible grace! What undeserved favor! Thank You for never denying me. _____

_____

_____

_____

_____

_____

_____

_____

_____

_____

_____

_____

DAY 82

King of the Mountain

Before You Begin

Read Luke 22:63–71

Stop and Consider

They all asked, "Are You, then, the Son of God?"
And He said to them, "You say that I am" (v. 70).

I feel like asking a question Jesus asked much earlier in His earthly life: "Who do people say that the Son of Man is?" (Matt. 16:13). _____

_____

_____

What are they actually doing and saying by proclaiming Christ to be much less than He really is? _____

_____

_____

_____

I remember a childhood game I tried to avoid at all costs. It was called King of the Mountain. The players established a high place of some kind as the "mountain." The "king" was the one who could defend his territory by kicking or pushing anyone who came near him. It was a mean game. But it was nothing compared to the real-life King of the Mountain contest that took place between Pilate, Herod, the self-promoting religious leaders . . . and the true King Jesus, the One and Only.

As you picture every moment of these "mock court" proceedings in Luke 22, don't lose sight of these words in verse 70: "Are you then the Son of God?" Imagine every event unfolding on a large-screen TV, and during the entire ordeal these words scroll boldly across the bottom of the scene: "The Son of God." The irony is this: the only reason Christ was standing in front of them was because He was exactly who they "tried" Him for being. Though His accusers couldn't see the truth for themselves, Christ was found guilty of being the Son of God. They would end up releasing the insurrectionist and crucifying the Savior of the world.

Aren't you thankful humanity can "try" Christ for being anything they choose, and yet He is who He is? No amount of disbelief can change Him or move Him. Why did the chief priests and teachers of the law disbelieve? Why couldn't they accept their Messiah? Because they wanted to be king of the mountain.

And so our Savior was stripped. Mocked. Spat upon. Struck . . . again and again. Flogged. Beyond recognition. The fullness of the Godhead bodily. The bright and morning Star. The Alpha and Omega. The anointed of the Lord. The beloved Son of God. The radiance of His Father's glory. The Light of the world. The Hope of glory. The Lily of the valley. The Prince of peace. The Seed of David. The Son of righteousness. The blessed and only potentate, the King of kings, and Lord of lords. Emmanuel. The With of God.

The most terrifying truth a mocking humanity will ever confront is that no matter how Jesus is belittled, He cannot be made little. He is the King of the mountain.

Praying God's Word Today

Sovereign Lord, though we have all been guilty of serving idols in our lives, thank You for continuing to draw us toward Your holy mountain, where the entire house of Israel—every one of Your chosen people—will serve You, and where You will accept our offerings of praise and service (Ezek. 20:39–40). You, Lord, are now—and forever will be—the King of the mountain.

DAY 83

The Nails

Before You Begin

Read Luke 23:26–31

Stop and Consider

A great multitude of the people followed Him, including
women who were mourning and lamenting Him (v. 27).

Our Jesus—our One and Only—is being led away to death. Join the women who are
"mourning" and "lamenting Him." What are you hearing? What are you feeling? _____

_____

_____

What are other things in life that we should be mourning and lamenting over? What
should be invoking our sorrow today? _____

_____

_____

_____

According to ancient custom, the cross, or at least the crossbeam, was placed upon the ground, then Christ was stretched out upon it. I cannot imagine being the one who actually targeted the nail to the proper place in the skin and struck the blow. Do you think he at all costs avoided Christ's eyes?

They probably secured His hands before His feet so that His arms would not flail when His feet were nailed. We often picture that the nail wounds were in the palms, but the delicate bones in the hands could not hold a victim to the cross. The nails were usually driven through the wrists. In Hebrew, the wrist was considered part of the hand rather than the arm.

Without becoming more graphic than necessary, crucifixion, almost always preceded by a near-to-death flogging, was unimaginably painful and inhumane. This kind of capital punishment was targeted as a deterrent for rebellious slaves and was forbidden to any Roman citizen, no matter how serious his crime. Crucifixion was a totally inhumane way for even the two criminals to die. But this was the King of glory! They took a hammer and nails to the "Word made flesh."

I want you to sit and "listen" to the sound of the hammer striking. I'm not trying to be melodramatic. I just want us to come as close as possible to being eyewitnesses. You don't have to open your eyes and "look," but I want you to open your spiritual ears and listen. Move close enough to hear the conversation of the marksman as he positions the nail at the wrist of Christ. You'll have to fight the crowd to get close enough. Then listen to the hammer hit the nail—several times at each hand and foot to make sure the nails are securely in place. I'm not trying to make you wince. I only want you to hear the sound as the nails are driven securely into the wood.

If you study the Old Testament prophecies of Jesus, you will find that they come in a dazzling variety of forms. In some places the predictions were clear. They obviously pointed to the coming Messiah. In other instances they were veiled. Join me now as we look at an absolutely fascinating passage—these words that apply so beautifully to Christ at

this moment. In their immediate sense, they were written about Eliakim, the palace super-intendent during the Assyrian invasion of Israel, but you can see their ultimate significance in terms of the cross of our Christ. In the passage God said,

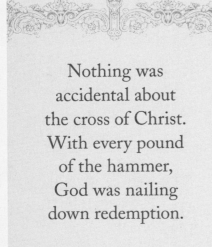

Nothing was accidental about the cross of Christ. With every pound of the hammer, God was nailing down redemption.

"I will clothe him with your robe and fasten your sash around him and hand your authority over to him. He will be a father to those who live in Jerusalem and to the house of Judah. I will place on his shoulder the key to the house of David; what he opens no one can shut, and what he shuts no one can open. I will drive him like a peg into a firm place; he will be a seat of honor for the house of his father" (Isa. 22:21–23).

Note how God said He would give His servant the key to the house of David, opening a door no one can shut. He said He would "drive him like a peg into a firm place." As unfathom-able as the process is to you and me, the cross was the means by which God chose to position Christ in the seat of honor for the house of His Father. The cross is the open door no man can shut.

Isaiah 22:23 says, "I will fasten him as a nail in a sure place" (KJV). The original word for "firm" in the NIV and "sure" in the KJV is *aman*: "in a transitive sense to make firm, to confirm . . . to stand firm; to be enduring; to trust."

Nothing was accidental about the cross of Christ. The Son of God was not suddenly overcome by the wickedness of man and nailed to a cross. Quite the contrary, the cross was the means by which the Son of God overcame the wickedness of man. To secure the keys to the house of David and open the door of salvation to all who would enter, God drove His Son like a nail in a sure place. A firm place. An enduring place.

As painful and horrendous as the pounding hammer sounds to our spiritual ears, Colossians 2:13–14 says that while we were dead in our sins, God made us alive with Christ. He "canceled the written code, with its regulations, that was against us and that stood opposed to us; he took it away, nailing it to the cross."

I will never fully grasp how such human atrocities occurred at the free will of humanity, while God used them to unfold His perfect, divine, and redemptive plan. Christ was nailed to the cross as the one perfect human. He was the fulfillment of the law in every way. When God drove His Son like a nail in a firm place, He took the written code, finally fulfilled in His Son, and canceled our debt to it. With every pound of the hammer, God was nailing down redemption.

"When I am lifted up from the earth, [I] will draw all men to myself" (John 12:32). How do you imagine those words rang in the disciples' minds when they finally understood what Jesus had meant? _____

_____

_____

_____

_____

_____

_____

PRAYING GOD'S WORD TODAY

Lord Jesus, as my heart breaks today, my love for You swells. For You emptied Yourself by assuming the form of a slave, taking on the likeness of men. And when You had come as a man, You humbled Yourself by becoming obedient to the point of death—even to death on a cross (Phil. 2:7–8). Obedient to Your Father. The final sacrifice for Your people. I give You all my praise and honor, Lord Jesus, my Savior. _____

_____

_____

_____

_____

_____

_____

_____

_____

_____

_____

_____

_____

_____

DAY 84

Father, Forgive Them

BEFORE YOU BEGIN
Read Luke 23:32–43

STOP AND CONSIDER

Jesus said, "Father, forgive them, because they do not know what they are doing" (v. 34).

Is there someone you've been withholding forgiveness from? What is the offence? What do you sense as you write it down again on paper? What are your reasons for holding on to it?

_____

_____

_____

What would forgiveness require of you? What did it require of Jesus? What would His advice be to you about how to handle it? _____

_____

_____

_____

As if the physical wounds Christ suffered were not enough, they were not the killers in crucifixion. Death crept in slowly through exhaustion and asphyxiation from an increasing inability to hold oneself up to draw breath. If you've ever experienced anything close to "excruciating" pain, can you imagine how difficult talking would be?

Regardless of how many times you've heard sermons preached on Christ's next words, don't hear them casually. The moment words formed on His tongue and His voice found volume, He said, "Father, forgive them, for they do not know what they are doing" (Luke 23:34).

Not "Father, consume them," but "Father, forgive them." This may be the most perfect statement spoken at the most perfect time since God gave the gift of language. As unimaginable as His request was, it was so fitting! If the cross is about anything at all, it is about forgiveness. Forgiveness of the most incorrigible and least deserving.

I don't believe the timing of the statement was meaningless. It was the first thing He said after they nailed Him to the cross and hoisted it into view. His immediate request for the Father's forgiveness sanctified the cross for its enduring work through all of time. His request baptized the crude wood for its divine purpose.

Please understand, the cross itself had no power. Neither was it ever meant to be an idol, but it represents something so divine and powerful that the apostle Paul said, "May I never boast except in the cross of our Lord Jesus Christ, through which the world has been crucified to me, and I to the world" (Gal. 6:14).

Dr. Luke was the only one God inspired to record the forgiveness statement. How appropriate that a physician would be the one to pen such healing words. Surely, in the days to come, many involved were haunted by their consciences. No doubt many in the crowd at the crucifixion were saved on the Day of Pentecost, since both events occurred in Jerusalem only weeks apart and on major feast days. The main reason to believe these were the same people, however, is because God doesn't ordinarily refuse the request of His Son.

Praying God's Word Today

I hear Your Word to me today, Father, as one of Your chosen ones, holy and loved: "Put on heartfelt compassion, kindness, humility, gentleness, and patience, accepting one another and forgiving one another if anyone has a complaint against another. Just as the Lord has forgiven you, so also you must forgive" (Col. 3:12–13). Yes, Lord Jesus—just as You did.

DAY 85

The Cost of the Cross

BEFORE YOU BEGIN
Read Matthew 27:45–54

STOP AND CONSIDER

At about three in the afternoon, Jesus cried out with a loud voice, "Elî, Elî, lemá sabachtháni?" that is, "My God, My God, why have You forsaken Me?" (v. 46).

Why was this a more pitiful cry than all the others He must have gasped in the process of His physical torture? _____

_____

_____

Deal with this reality: every unbeliever is truly living in separation from almighty God. How does that affect your urgency to show them Jesus? _____

_____

_____

_____

The curtain drops on our scene in the form of darkness, which lasted three hours. The Light of the world was about to be extinguished, if only for a brief time. Just before He breathed His last, Jesus cried out with a loud voice, "Father, into your hands I commit my spirit" (Luke 23:46). How appropriate that He would use His last breaths to utter the trust upon which His entire life had rested.

But I'm not sure we can properly appreciate those words of faith unless we consider the ones spoken by Him only moments before. I believe this cry, "My God, my God, why have you forsaken me?" marked the exact moment when the sins of all humanity—past, present, and future—were heaped upon Christ and the full cup of God's wrath poured forth. Somehow I believe that to bear the sin, Jesus also had to bear the separation. Though Christ had to suffer the incomparable agony of separation from the fellowship of His Father while sin was judged, I am moved that He breathed His last breath with full assurance of His Father's trustworthiness. The human body of the life-giver hung lifeless. It was finished. He gave up His last human breath so He never had to give up on humanity.

Several years ago, I had the privilege of participating in a solemn assembly of 30,000 college students gathered on a huge field in Memphis, Tennessee. After we heard a powerful message about the cross, two young men began to walk down the hill carrying a large wooden cross. The two students, bent under the weight, carried the heavy cross through the crowd to a place just in front of the platform and then erected it as a visual aid. We couldn't possibly have planned what happened next.

Students began running to the cross with an urgency I can neither possibly describe nor recall without sobs. They sprinted from every direction through the crowd. Their sobs echoed in the open air. They lifted the cross out of the ground and began to pass it with their hands lifted high above their heads all over the crowd. They passed it from hands to hands all over the crowd and up the hill. I am covered with chills as I recall the scene when the repentant found refuge in the shadow of the cross.

In our sophistication and familiarity, have we been away too long? Run to the cross.

PRAYING GOD'S WORD TODAY

You Yourself have said to us, "I will never leave you or forsake you." Therefore, we may boldly say, "The Lord is my helper; I will not be afraid. What can man do to me?" (Heb. 13:5–6).

DAY 86

He Is Risen!

BEFORE YOU BEGIN
Read Luke 23:50–56, Luke 24:1–8

STOP AND CONSIDER
The women were terrified and bowed to the ground. "Why are you
looking for the living among the dead?" asked the men (v. 5).

Try to recapture a moment from your life when you went from deep disappointment to
sheer elation—all in the same day, or at least in a short time span. _____

_____

_____

If you had been one of the women who first saw Jesus resurrected, how do you think you
would have reacted? _____

_____

_____

_____

How the Sabbath hours must have dragged for these women. They had prepared the spices and perfumes but were forced to rest on the Sabbath. They had come with Jesus from Galilee, so we can assume they were guests in others' homes. Surely the time seemed to be an eternity. Women two thousand years ago were not so unlike we are today. We want to do something. Feeling needed is sometimes the very thing that keeps a woman going. For months they "had followed him and cared for his needs" (Mark 15:41). Now all that was left to do was to serve Him in memorial. They needed to get to the tomb and do the one last thing they could for their Lord.

As the moments crawled by, I'm sure these women recounted with horror the last few days' events. Surely at times they sat in silence, each one weeping in painful solitude as she remembered every encounter with Him. Jesus had a way of making a person feel like the apple of His eye. He still does.

The women "rested" through a Sabbath dusk that frustratingly gave way to night. More waiting. They probably never slept a wink and were on their way to the tomb before a cock could crow. John 20:1, spotlighting Mary Magdalene, tells us "it was still dark."

Mark tells us that the women were hoping the officials would allow someone to roll away the stone so they could apply the spices and perfumes to the body. To their astonishment, they saw that the "very large" stone had been rolled away. The women had no way of knowing at that moment what Matthew 28:2–4 records. I love the wording in Matthew 28:2: "An angel of the Lord came down from heaven and, going to the tomb, rolled back the stone and sat on it." Can you fathom the angels' horror when humans mocked, spat on, beat, flogged, and crucified the Son of God?

Imagine the joy of the angel whose thunderous arrival caused the ground to shake. God chose him to be the one who rolled back the stone—not to *free* Jesus, but to reveal Him already missing! Can you picture the angel's gleaming face as he perched on that stone? The guards were so afraid that they shook and became like dead men. The grave-yard *needed* a few folks acting like dead men, since a number of the formerly dead were

suddenly walking the streets (see Matt. 27:52–53). I'm about to have to shout hallelujah! The women entered the tomb, but they did not find the body.

Acts 2:24 tells us exactly why Christ was raised from the dead: "God raised him from the dead, freeing him from the agony of death, because it was impossible for death to keep its hold on him." Some things are simply impossible—and death keeping its hold on Jesus is one of them.

Mind you, the women didn't yet understand. Luke 24:4 tells us "while they were wondering about this, suddenly two men in clothes that gleamed like lightning stood beside them." John's version hints at these two celestial ambassadors' assignment. He tells us the two angels were seated where Jesus' body had been, "one at the head and the other at the foot" (John 20:12).

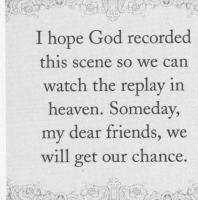

I hope God recorded this scene so we can watch the replay in heaven. Someday, my dear friends, we will get our chance.

Quite possibly, these angels also guarded the body of Jesus while it lay "in state" in the sepulcher. The Old Testament tabernacle contained a marvelous picture foreshadowing this moment. The ark of the covenant represented the very presence of God. In Exodus 25:17–22, the very specific instructions for the "mercy seat" (KJV) or "atonement cover" (NIV) on the ark of the covenant demanded the cherubim to be in exactly that position. Do you see the picture? No, I can't be dogmatic that the cherubim prefigured the angels at Christ's head and feet—but I am personally convinced. Jesus has always been the means by which God would "meet with" humanity (Exod. 25:22).

If the cherubim prefigured the angels in the tomb, can you imagine how they guarded the body through the wait? With their wings overshadowing Him, they faced each other, looking toward the cover. Picture their reactions when the glorified body of Jesus sat up from the death shroud and walked out of the tomb, right through the rock. Wouldn't you have loved to hear as Christ thanked them for their service?

Glory to God! Though the news echoed throughout the heavenlies at the moment of Christ's resurrection, the angels probably longed for God to turn on their volume in the earthly realm and announce it to the mortals. At the sight of the angels, the women fell on their faces. The celestial guards announced to them, "Why do you look for the living among the dead?" The what? The living! "He is not here; he has risen!" (Luke 24:5–6).

Oh, glorious, merciful, omnipotent God! He is risen indeed! I cherish the next five words of the angels: "Remember how he told you" (v. 6). Beloved, have you forgotten something He told you? Christ, our Lord, is faithful to His promises. If you're not presently "seeing" Him at work in your situation, do not live as if He's lifeless and you're hopeless. Believe Him and expect Him to reveal His resurrection power to you!

I ask again, giving you room to respond—"Have you forgotten something He told you?" As you journey through your present path or problem, is there a word of Scripture you heard in the past that rings with much deeper truth and perspective for you now? _____

_____

_____

_____

_____

_____

_____

Praying God's Word Today

O Father, help me grasp again today at least a portion of the immeasurable greatness of Your power, made available now to us who believe, according to the working of Your vast strength. You demonstrated this power in Your Son by raising Him from the dead and seating Him at Your right hand in the heavens, far above every ruler, authority, power, and dominion (Eph. 1:19–20). Hallelujah! Your power in my life is great!

DAY 87

In a Woman's Voice

Before You Begin
Read Luke 24:9–12

Stop and Consider
Mary Magdalene, Joanna, Mary the mother of James, and the other women with them were telling the apostles these things (v. 10).

What are some tasks and services done in Christ's name that are often more effectively performed by women than men? _____

_____

_____

Which of these do you feel the most called to and equipped for? _____

_____

_____

_____

_____

If I may say with a chuckle, one possible reason God chose to reveal the resurrection first to women is because He can trust us to get the word out! Telling what we've been told is our specialty! However, nothing can deflate the spirits of an enthusiastic woman like an apprehensive audience. Luke 24:11 records that the apostles "did not believe the women, because their words seemed to them like nonsense."

Sisters, don't be insulted by this scene in Luke 24:11. Rather, be blessed that God was up to something awesome even in this seemingly insignificant detail. You see, "the witness of women was not [even] acceptable in that day."[11] They couldn't testify as witnesses.

Now isn't this just like our Jesus! He threatened the status quo in countless ways, not the least of which concerned women. He invited them into Bible class (see Luke 10:39) after they had spent centuries learning what little Scripture they could from their husbands. He honored their service during a time in which men were the only ones who ministered publicly (see Mark 15:41). He healed, forgave, delivered, and made whole the very ones society shunned. Women of ill repute.

Appointing these women as the first to share the news of Jesus' resurrection was a definite "custom shaker." Jesus knew the apostles wouldn't believe them, but perhaps He felt that the pending discovery of their authenticity would breed a fresh respect. After all, at the first roll call in the post-ascension New Testament church, you'll see women listed as part of the first New Testament cell group (see Acts 1:13–14).

For centuries the synagogue had kept men and women separate. Suddenly they would be working, praying, and worshiping shoulder-to-shoulder. Christ built His church on a foundation of mutual respect. Don't misunderstand. Christ wasn't prioritizing women over men. He simply took the ladder down to the basement where society had lowered women. And with His nail-scarred hands, He lifted them to a place of respect and credibility.

The last thing we women should want to do in the body of Christ is to take men's places. They have far too much responsibility for my taste! But by all means, let's take *our* places! We have also been called to be credible witnesses of the Lord Jesus Christ.

PRAYING GOD'S WORD TODAY

Lord, how grateful I am that You have assigned certain roles in Your order of things for men and for women. Our differences are reflections of Your creative glory. And yet I am so grateful, too, that each of us who have been baptized into Christ have put on Christ. There is no more Jew or Greek, slave or free, male or female, for You have made us all one in Christ Jesus (Gal. 3:27–28). Use us in whatever ways You desire, but unite us in our shared fellowship as saints.

DAY 88

Snapshots with Jesus

BEFORE YOU BEGIN
Read Luke 24:13–35

STOP AND CONSIDER

He asked them, "What is this dispute that you're having with each other as you are walking?" And they stopped walking and looked discouraged (v. 17).

If we could see your face right now—your expression of faith—what would it look like?

_____

_____

What is the typical impression most people get when they see a Christian today? Just from the look on our face, what would they imply about the difference faith can make? _____

_____

_____

_____

_____

Imagine that God has decorated your mansion in glory with a number of framed pictures of you and Christ. The pictures capture the two of you during momentous earthly occasions. You could not see Him with your eyes, but He was there every moment in living color. Hopefully, we've each walked with Him long enough to have a few treasured photos with expressions suggesting we chose to see with the eyes of faith rather than the eyes of humanity. I can almost imagine Christ sitting around heaven with small groups of us, pulling out the photo album, pointing out a few sour expressions. Picture us covering our faces with good-humored embarrassment, turning as red as beets.

No doubt the still shot of Cleopas in Luke 24:17 is one that would spur a little good-natured, heavenly ribbing. Christ, however, didn't find it nearly so amusing this side of heaven. Note that the events surrounding Christ's crucifixion were so well publicized, Cleopas implied that Jesus must have been a visitor to be unaware of the recent happenings. He then proceeded to tell Christ . . . about Himself! Can you imagine being in Cleopas's sandals? Wouldn't you hope you got the facts straight?

If Christ had been a teacher grading Cleopas on his oral report, what grade do you think He would've given him? If I were doing the grading, I wouldn't have subtracted points until the "kicker" in Luke 24:21: "But we had hoped that he was the one." Picture the downcast face, the sagging posture. Listen to the tone in his voice. For a clue, see Christ's indignant response in Luke 24:25: "He said to them, 'How foolish you are, and how slow of heart to believe all that the prophets have spoken!'" Cleopas seemed to be saying, "We had hoped . . . but He let us down."

The Word of God often couples a downcast soul with feelings of hopelessness. In Greek the word for "hope" encompasses far more than wishful thinking. It means "confident expectation." Christ told His followers what to "expect" and reminded them that a victorious ending would follow the tragic means. When Christ gives us His Word, He wants us to live in absolute expectation of it, trusting that whether it happens sooner or later, it will happen.

Cleopas and his friend had allowed the very evidence that could have ignited them with hope to make them hopeless instead. Remember now—the women had shared the testimony that Christ was alive. I realize I'm taking the next statement out of context, but I get a kick out of Cleopas's words in Luke 24:22: "In addition, some of our women amazed us." There you have it. Women are amazing. It's absolutely scriptural. Of course, *amazing* can mean many things. The most common colloquialism we have that matches the word for *amazing* is to say something has "blown our minds." I blow Keith's mind all the time—but it's not always something for me to be proud of. Sometimes he just stands there and gives me that "she's blonder than she pays to be" look.

> Can you imagine how ridiculous we look with our hopeless, downcast faces while the immortal Son of God is standing right beside us?

Christ clearly showed His displeasure over the men's disbelief. He rebuked them, but He followed the rebuke with some of the most amazing moments in Scripture: "Beginning with Moses and all the Prophets, he explained to them what was said in all the Scriptures concerning himself" (v. 27). What I would give to hear that comprehensive dissertation! Christ began with the books of Moses, went straight through the prophets, and explained what was said in all the Scriptures concerning Himself. Part of heaven for me will be hearing a replay of this sermon! The entire Old Testament was written about or toward Christ. Imagine Jesus Himself explaining the hundreds of ways the Scriptures predict and prepare for His coming. I could teach on this subject for hours, and I don't know even a fraction of the ways Christ is taught in the Old Testament.

Luke's use of "explained" (v. 27) in reference to Christ's teaching means "to interpret, translate. To explain clearly and exactly." I can't wait to know exactly what some Scriptures mean. Unlike me, Christ never had to say, "I think . . ." or "I believe this means . . ." He knew. What a Bible lesson those two men heard! A lesson that would have taken forty

years of wilderness wanderings for me, Christ delivered with glorious precision over a few Emmaus miles. No wonder the two men hated to part with Jesus! "Jesus acted as if he were going farther. But they urged him strongly, 'Stay with us'" (vv. 28–29).

Don't you love the part in a movie when the surprise is revealed? We have now arrived at that climactic moment. Allow me to set the stage for you. The men invited Jesus into one of their homes. A simple meal was prepared. They reclined at the table. Christ took the role as server. He broke the bread and called down divine favor through a benediction. He handed each of them a portion of the small loaf. As if the veil of the Holy of Holies was torn again before their very eyes, they recognized Him! Then He disappeared.

Talk about a photo I want to see in a heavenly album! Can you imagine those expressions? I have a feeling "downcast" wouldn't be an adequate description.

What pictures would you like to see on the walls of your mansion in glory? How do you hope you look in them? _____

_____

_____

_____

_____

_____

_____

PRAYING GOD'S WORD TODAY

Why am I so depressed and downcast? Why this turmoil within me? I will put my hope in You, Lord, for I will still praise You, my Savior and my God (Ps. 43:5).

DAY 89

A Frightening Peace

BEFORE YOU BEGIN
Read Luke 24:36–49

STOP AND CONSIDER

He said to them, "Peace to you!" But they were startled and
terrified and thought they were seeing a ghost (vv. 36–37).

Has Jesus ever scared you? Has being in His presence ever made you feel nervous, wary,
or unsettled? _____

_____

_____

When it happens, what does it tell you about Him? What does it tell you about yourself?

_____

_____

_____

_____

I have to laugh out loud from the delightful irony that Christ's greeting of peace nearly scared the disciples to death (see Luke 24:37). John 20:19 helps explain why Christ's surprise visit incited such fear. The disciples were locked in for fear of the Jews.

Luke 24:37 translates two very strong original words to describe the terror of the disciples. Suffice it to say, they could not have been more frightened. I think they would have run for their lives if they could have moved. Notice that just minutes earlier they were cheering, "It is true!" But somehow when they came face-to-face with Jesus, the sight was almost more than they could bear.

I delight in knowing our future will be somewhat similar. You and I have banked our entire Christian lives on the fact that Jesus is very much alive, yet I have a feeling when we actually behold Him, it will only be eternal life that keeps us from dropping like dead men. Christ responded to the fright of His disciples by asking, "Why are you troubled, and why do doubts rise in your minds?" The original word for "troubled" implies a sudden disturbance of all sorts of emotions.

The original word for "doubts" in Luke 24:38 is *dialogismos*. You see in it the word *dialogue*. The Greek word means "thoughts and directions" and can also mean "debate." I think the disciples' minds went on instant overload, dialoguing all sorts of debates between what their eyes suddenly saw and what their brains could not rationalize. I can almost hear Christ saying, "Boys, you don't have a mental file already prepared to stick this information in. This one won't compute intellectually. Quit trying. Just behold and believe."

Christ's willingness to continue to draw us to belief totally astounds me. At no time did He say, "You bunch of idiots! I'm sick of trying to talk you into believing me!" When the sight of Him wasn't enough, Jesus said, "Look at my hands and my feet. It is I myself! Touch me and see; a ghost does not have flesh and bones, as you see I have" (v. 39).

We have often seen His hands through constant provision and glorious intervention. We have often seen His feet as He's gone before us. Surely we have beheld the hands and feet of Christ with eyes of faith. Let us not be afraid, but only believe.

PRAYING GOD'S WORD TODAY

God of peace, may You who brought up from the dead our Lord Jesus—the great Shepherd of the sheep—with the blood of the everlasting covenant, equip us with all that is good to do Your will, working in us what is pleasing in Your sight through Jesus Christ, to whom be glory forever and ever (Heb. 13:20–21).

DAY 90

We Beheld His Glory

Before You Begin
Read Luke 24:50–53

Stop and Consider

While He was blessing them, He left them and was carried up to heaven.
After worshiping Him, they returned to Jerusalem with great joy (vv. 51–52).

Try to put yourself on that hillside. See your Lord being carried up in glory. Feel your heart beating hard, not sure what to do next. What is it like? What are you thinking? _____

_____

_____

Think back on some experiences you've had with Christ that should have been unforgettable but have somehow slipped from your memory. What do you need to remember about who He is and what He's done for you? _____

_____

_____

_____

Luke's Gospel pen, filled by the ink of the Spirit for twenty-four glorious chapters, appropriately runs dry on a priceless scene. A small band of motley men, whose lives had been turned every which way but loose by Jesus of Nazareth, strained for their last earthly glimpse of Him.

Thirty-three years earlier, the feet of God toddled their first visible prints on earth, a young mother's footprints chasing close behind. The walk grew rough, the path strewn with stones and thorns. Now God incarnate stepped off this planet with feet scarred and bruised. As God predicted at the fall, the ancient serpent struck Christ's heel, but on the day He ascended, all things were under Christ's feet. Jesus Christ walked the way of humanity so that humanity could walk the way of God. How beautiful the feet that brought good news.

Not one of those disciples was sorry He had come their way. Their losses were incalculable. Most of their friends. Much of their family. Their jobs. The blessings of their fathers. Physical safety. And now, a leader they could see. Yet they left the Mount of Olives with great joy, continually praising God, for their ordinary lives had been interrupted by glory.

The sufferings of this world simply could not compare to the glory He had revealed to them. It sustained and swelled them long after the visible became invisible. You and I are the spiritual descendants of Peter, James, John, and all the others who offered their lives, not for what they thought or what they hoped, but for what they knew. Whom they knew. Our faith is based on fact, beloved. Never let anyone convince you otherwise.

Jesus the One and Only—the title is His forever. He was the One and Only long before He breathed a soul into humanity, and He will continue to be the One and Only long after the last soul has been judged. He is changeless. But you and I were destined for change. So determined is God to transform us, we cannot draw near Him and remain the same. May our tenure on this planet be characterized by one simple word . . . *Jesus!*

PRAYING GOD'S WORD TODAY

I praise You, Lord Jesus, for becoming flesh and taking up residence among us. We have observed Your glory, that glory as the One and Only Son from the Father, full of grace and truth. Indeed, we have all received grace after grace from Your fullness (John 1:14, 16). So thank You for revealing yourself to me afresh through these ninety days with You. And from this day forward, may my life be an ever-increasing reflection of Your glory. _____

_____

_____

_____

_____

_____

_____

_____

_____

_____

_____

_____

_____

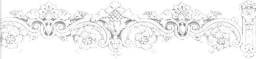

ENDNOTES

1. Beth Moore, *Things Pondered: From the Heart of a Lesser Woman* (Nashville: B&H Publishing Group, 1997), 7.

2. Robert H. Stein, *Jesus the Messiah: A Survey of the Life of Christ* (Downers Grove, Ill.: InterVarsity Press, 1996), 106.

3. Dr. Chuck Lynch, *I Should Forgive, But . . .* (Nashville: Word, 1998), 33–34.

4. Matthew Henry, *Matthew Henry's Commentary on the Whole Bible* (New York: Fleming H. Revell), 634.

5. Francis Frangipane, *Exposing the Accuser of the Brethren* (Cedar Rapids, Iowa: Arrow Publications, 1991), 37.

6. Spiros Zodhiates, ed. *The Hebrew-Greek Key Study Bible* (Chattanooga, Tenn.: AMG Publishers, 1966), 1647.

7. Jim Cymbala, *Fresh Wind, Fresh Fire* (Grand Rapids, Mich.: Zondervan, 1997), 19.

8. Kevin Howard and Marvin Rosenthal, *The Feasts of the Lord* (Orlando, Fla.: Zion's Hope, Inc., 1997), 55.

9. Ibid., 57.

10. Colin Brown, *The New International Dictionary of the New Testament Theology* (Grand Rapids, Mich.: Zondervan, 1986), 614.

11. Frank E. Gaebelein, ed. *The Expositor's Bible Commentary* (Grand Rapids, Mich.: Zondervan, 1984), 1049.